MANNING
ON
DECOUPAGE

Hiram Manning

Dover Publications Inc.
New York

Published in Canada by General Publishing Company,
Ltd., 30 Lesmill Road, Don Mills, Toronto, Ontario.
Published in the United Kingdom by Constable and Com-
pany, Ltd., 10 Orange Street, London WC2H 7EG.

This Dover edition, first published in 1980, is an un-
abridged and slightly corrected republication of the work
originally published in 1969. This edition is published by
special arrangement with Hearthside Press, Inc., publishers
of the original edition.

International Standard Book Number: 0-486-24028-2
Library of Congress Catalog Card Number: 80-66224

Manufactured in the United States of America
Dover Publications, Inc.
180 Varick Street
New York, N.Y. 10014

This book is dedicated to a pair of wonderfully creative hands, now stilled, those of my mother, Maybelle Manning.

FOREWORD

Last Christmas I received a beautiful present. Clare Boothe Luce sent me a nest of boxes that my mother had decoupaged for her some eighteen years ago. It started me thinking about my first exposure to that art form.

In the fall of 1946, I had just returned to New York from a stint on the sound stages of Hollywood, filled with a burning ambition to be a "real" actress. And that, to me, meant "live" theatre— Broadway.

Captain Hiram Manning had just returned from a five-year tour of duty on the battlefields of Europe. He, too, was filled with a burning ambition—peace—as well as with a compelling desire to decoupage everything in sight. In fact, I often feel that when Hi meets someone his mind is sizing them up as a subject for decoupage. (In gold leaf, maybe, with a chinoiserie design, or possibly red lacquer and Venetian figures might be better?) I don't want to give you the impression that Hi Manning is a ghoul; simply that in his mind *anything* of natural material is a fit subject for his art of beautification.

In those early days of the revival of decoupage—and it had to be revived because there were no sources available to us—we latched onto any thing or object at hand. Old corroded tin trays, beat-up furniture, cigar boxes supplied by Mac Kriendler of "21"—you name it, it got decoupaged. Hi and his enchanting mother, Maybelle, bewitched everyone with their enthusiasm.

And so it began, the Mannings leading and the Cobb family trailing (willing, if not very apt, pupils). As a matter of fact, in those days Hi and Maybelle weren't so red-hot either, because so much had been lost or forgotten. So an old magazine, a seed catalog—anything—was cut, designed and glued. Any and all glues and varnishes were eagerly tried, while Hi desperately tried to recall and re-create the original French formulas. I can still smell his pots of witches' brew cooking on the stove!

How times have changed from those sad little messes with bubbles in the varnish, and black print from the reverse side bleeding through a badly glued pink rose, to the exquisite quality of design and workmanship that now comes from the Manning Studio in Boston.

One of my happiest memories is that of the Cobbs and Mannings on our porch in Colebrook, Connecticut: my grandmother, "Moie" [my adored Moie, the late Mrs. Irvin S. Cobb.—Author] in her custom-made blue jeans and wobbling pince-nez, working like a Trojan in her beloved garden; my mother, Buff, howling that her mayonnaise was not mayonnaising (that's 'cause she couldn't cook); me, making mint concoctions, mostly juleps; Maybelle, laughing and telling funny stories, her eyes on her work, scissors going constantly, cutting out those exquisite, intricate designs; and Hi, looking up from coloring prints, pencil in hand, just long enough to cock an eye at me and admonish, "Put in more bourbon, you phony Southern Belle!" (You see, the two families were "swamp Yankees"—translation: born in the South, living in New England.) I didn't quite qualify, having been born in Italy and having a Yankee father.

The Mannings were never idle or unproductive, and were a most remarkable team. It is not too often that you see a mother and son who work together successfully. More unusual still, they truly liked each other and respected each other as totally separate people.

Now the team is no more; my darling Maybelle is gone. But the work goes on. Hi, as he always has, creates beauty and teaches and lectures on decoupage all over the country. And now, he gives us this book, which is the sum of their combined experiences and the experiments that led to all the beautiful decoupage objects made by them and by all their pupils, those lucky people who have had the unique and rewarding experience of working with—and more important—of knowing, the Mannings.

BUFF COBB MARTIN

Le Touché

ACKNOWLEDGMENTS

For twenty-five years I have wanted to write this book for all you real *découpeurs;* but I have never felt I knew enough. I still feel that way in spite of constantly being told by friends and pupils that I know more about decoupage than anyone living. I guess in an odd way I do, and I wish to thank all those who kept bolstering my faltering ego.

This book is written in my own peculiar style. I write for you as I teach. I wish to talk *with* you, not *at* you, and to share and pass on to you all that I know. If at times I seem to "bark" at you, bear with me. I don't want you to make all the terrible mistakes I did, so whenever I tell you to do something or not to do it, the instruction has been evolved through my own blood, sweat and tears.

I wish first to thank with all my heart that wonderful, unique family who so generously passed the art on to me at St. Lô in France. Their personal tragedy was as great as that of their city, which was utterly destroyed in the Normandy invasion of World War II. I want them to know, wherever they are, that I am passing on what they so exquisitely passed on to me. *Salut!*

I also wish to thank my mother, whose memory still inspires me, and all my friends and pupils from whom I learn daily and who so generously contributed their cherished decoupage to illustrate this book.

CONTENTS

ILLUSTRATIONS

The photographs of decoupage shown in the book were all designed and/or executed at the Manning Studio of Decoupage in Boston, under the supervision and tutelage of Maybelle and Hiram Manning, unless otherwise indicated. The actual decoupage was done by the person whose name appears at the end of each caption.

COLOR PLATES

Front cover.
Small bombé three-drawer commode, front view; 26″ high x 19″ wide. Pale Venetian blue ground; borders in Venetian blue with lapis lazuli accents, and moldings in burnished white water gold leaf. Decoupage in 18th Century Palette; cupids in Sanguine; cartouche scrolls in golden green. Hiram Manning. In the author's collection.

Inside front cover.
I. Pendant Bristol egg on natural ground with a decoupage of hand-colored prints by Raphael in Full 18th Century Palette. Brass stand, 12″ high. Mrs. W. James Moore.

II. Poodle chaise, 21″ long x 14″ wide x 23″ high, modeled after Mme. de Pompadour's copy of her own bed made for her little dog "Plon." Decoupage of 18th Century figures, cupids and scrolls from the "Garden Fantasy" in Full 18th Century Palette, inlaid with mother-of-pearl, on ground of Chinese apricot with bronzed gilt borders. Inside, cupids and flowers on ground of celadon blue. Cushions of Chinese apricot velvet. Curtains of yellow taffeta with blue silk fringe. Flanked on either side with gold roses in miniature bronze doré urns. Five generations of dogs have used it, including the author's present one, "Missie," a cairn terrier. The Mannings; in the author's collection.

III. Gold and peach tray, 30″ long, designed and executed by Hiram Manning. In the author's collection.

IV. Bombé box, decoupaged with prints by Raphael, in Full Palette on two-toned marbleized ground. Hiram Manning. In the author's collection.

V. Nest of tables, 15″ x 12″ x 22″. Decoupage of French scrolls and flowers in pinks, lavenders and yellows, on black jade ground. Inlaid at corners with mother-of-pearl. Jean R. Onwood, Cohasset, Mass.

Inside back cover.

VI. Early 18th Century (1735) Venetian *scrivania* (secretary desk) 9½′ high, with deep madder red ground, black borders, and gold scrolls. Decoupage of carnival scenes, scenes of Venice, and trophies of frivolities (masks, wigs, fans, powder puffs and patch boxes), with a running story of a flirtation: young wife, old husband; boy meets girl; old man drags her home by the ear. In the author's collection.

VII. Breakfast cabinet in the Biedermeier manner with pair of matching chairs (one shown). Decoupage of old valentine flowers, lavishly inset with mother-of-pearl, on black ground. Cabinet lined with pale lime green velvet. The Mannings, for the late Mrs. George Skakel, now in the possession of her daughter, Mrs. George Terrien, Greenwich, Conn.

VIII. Eight-foot screen in the Mogul manner. Cartouches of hand-colored Pillement chinoiserie scrolls and flowers, with pre-colored birds and butterflies. Large Gould tropical birds at top collaged on paper-mache, with one, alas, missing: a rather tragic example of not enough varnish to protect it, although it can and will be repaired. Designed by the Mannings; executed by Mrs. William Gillespie, Syracuse, N.Y.

Back cover.

LEFT: Round snuff box. Collage of paper-mache of Boucher cupids in Sanguine Palette, under varnish, on Sèvres pink ground. Designed and executed by Mrs. J. Verser Conner, Louisville, Ky. CENTER: Bombé box. Natural ground of honey pine with decoupage of baroque cupids and scrolls of wheat and flowers in Grisaille Palette. Mrs. Conner. RIGHT: Box en tombeau, or tomb-shaped, with gold feet; decoupage of 18th Century figures and interlaced scrolls in shot silk colors, on ground of lapis lazuli paper, cut in small cloud shapes and applied. Mrs. Conner.

The drawings used at the end of the Foreword and Chapters 9, 12, 19, and 20 are from *The Five Senses of Nature* by Jean Pillement.

DECOUPAGE: SOME PRELIMINARIES

1. *Towards a definition.*

Before we explore the origins of decoupage, let's try to settle the matter of what it is—and what it isn't.

I've tried to put it this way: basically, decoupage is the assembling and composing of many unrelated paper cutouts into a composite whole.

This covers a lot of territory. A decoupage can be under varnish; or under glass with *no* varnish; or on *top* of glass, porcelain or any variety of surfaces, with varnish then added; etc. The possibilities are really infinite: you can decoupage (I'm using the word as a verb as well as a noun) anything from a matchbox to an entire room—walls, floors and ceiling included—but just because you've colored, cut and stuck something on someplace doesn't mean it's a decoupage. Paint dabbled on canvas doesn't make a painting either—although that's been tried, too!

No, with decoupage, as with other media, it's the combination of, first, craftsmanship; second, the concept of the artist; and finally, his or her inherent artistry that transforms the product of a given technique into "something more."

And in the case of decoupage, the question arises, are we entitled to call the end result "art"? Let's think about that for a moment.

"Art" surely includes more than a canvas hung on a wall with a frame around it—although this seems to be an all-too-frequent definition today. In his book *Art Treasures of the Metropolitan,* the late Francis Henry Taylor, the director of New York's Metropolitan Museum of Art, comments that this tendency to use the word "art" as a synonym for painting is a fairly recent development. He states that one of the great tasks of his museum is to combat this restrictive concept, and his book illustrations show art ". . . in the form of stone, steel, bronze, wood, wool (tapestries, etc.), and   *a dozen substances that are not pigment on a flat surface."* (The italics are my own.)

So why can't we include cut paper? Mr. Taylor did; when he saw the decoupages done by my mother and me, he called them "fine art"—a statement I'll treasure always, as he wasn't a man given to loose compliments.

Back then, to the vexing but fascinating problem of the thin hairline that separates craft from art. What is the "something more" I spoke of earlier?

Not an easy question to answer, but this much we can say with certainty: all arts start out as crafts, but not all crafts become fine art.

First comes craft. Cellini was a goldsmith; Michelangelo a stone mason; Peter Carl Fabergé a jeweler—all "craftsmen" to begin with. Each transcended his craft, but each first *knew* his craft, backwards and forwards. Only then was he free to express himself as an artist. If Michelangelo hadn't mastered every facet of stone-carving, we'd have no "David"; if he hadn't known the craft of fresco (applying pigment to plaster), there would be no Sistine Chapel ceiling.

And here, perhaps, is where I can help you—not to be an artist, as this is the "something more" that can't be taught—but to perfect the mastery of your craft, so that you'll then be free to express yourself to the fullest extent of your own artistic capacity.

Yes, decoupage requires craft. The finished result can be no better than any one of its several stages. First, it must be beautifully designed, in harmony with the shape and quality of the piece, or object, it's done on; subsequently, it must be beautifully colored, cut, glued, varnished and finished, until the interplay between these various stages produces a glowing, completed entity. Then you'll have a work of art, perhaps—or, if the "something more" just isn't there, at least a fine piece of exquisite craftsmanship. Mess up just one stage—say, the cutting—and no matter how beautifully designed and executed your finished piece, it'll still be bad cutting. I've seen quite a bit of true decoupage, done by gifted people, but poorly finished or colored. These same people could produce superb pieces if the proper techniques and methods were made available to them; they are the ones I hope to help.

Back to our definition, then: decoupage is paper that has been colored, cut, assembled and glued *according to one's own design.* Your bits of cut paper are what bricks are to an architect or pigments to a painter: they're your means to an end: your own design. Not anyone else's; decoupage is not copying. Use your cuttings to create, and you'll have a true decoupage.

The other allied paper arts—folded paper, collage, montage, vue d'optique, moulage, etc.—can form part of a decoupage. Even as separate entities, they're still members of the family.

What about materials that aren't paper at all? There are two answers to this one. Strictly speaking, assemblages of wood, shell, beads, cloth etc. are *not decoupage;* they are, rather, marquetry, shellwork, beadwork, appliqué, or whatever. But a decoupage, primarily composed of cuts of paper, can *include,* for aesthetic effect, the occasional use of other substances such as mother-of-pearl or bits of fabric.

2. *Origins and history, of sorts.*

Where did decoupage come from? Is it something new? Far from it—but its exact date of origin remains a moot question. I've seen several examples of very old Chinese decoupage (poticho-

1. *Pair of extremely rare old Chinese silver mirrors under glass. Mirrors are polished silver; glass is coated with figures in gold-embroidered silk from ancient Imperial robes. When the robes rotted from age, figures were cut out, salvaged, and mounted on mirror which was then put under hand-blown glass in red lacquer frames. In author's collection.*

mania) done on glazed earthenware and lacquered. And I do possess a pair of centuries-old Chinese pictures composed of cuttings from extremely ancient silk imperial robes, glued on silver under glass (see Plate 1). I also have a Persian box that dates back to approximately 1400, covered in paper miniatures applied on a paper tortoiseshell ground. Other prized early samples include a few card boxes that may well be Italian in origin, as Italy is where I bought them. They're composed of hundreds of bits of paper, cut and glued to resemble fine inlaid wood, and their style leads me to date them from the 16th century.

But decoupage, as we know it today, had its great apogee in the 18th century. We've reason to believe that it began in Venice, when the vogue for painted and decorated furniture swept all before it, and that from there it wended its way north to France.

William M. Odum, in his *History of Italian Furniture,* published in 1919, finds the origin "uncertain." He quotes from an early 18th century letter from Mme. Aissé, as follows:

"We are here in the height of a new passion for cutting up

colored engravings . . . . Every lady, great and small, is cutting away. These cuttings are pasted on sheets of pasteboard and then varnished. We make wall panels, screens, and fireboards of them. There are books and engravings that cost up to 100 lire, and women are mad enough to cut up engravings worth 100 lire apiece. If this fashion continues, they will cut up Raphaels!" (See Plate 2 which uses *prints* of Raphael.)

Decoupage, all right! But bear in mind that Venice had already been producing magnificent pieces of decoupaged furniture. One thing is certain: the 18th century vogue was rampant in both countries.

2. Octagonal pedestal table, 25" high, with concealed door. Ground of lapis lazuli with orange and white marbleized top. Decoupage of Raphael prints from the loggia of the Vatican library. Hiram Manning. In author's collection.

The Italian name for decoupage is an oddity in itself: *l'arte del povero* or "poor man's art." When the painted-furniture industry in guild-dominated Venice was at its zenith, the customary practice was this: well-known artists would create original designs, which were then sketched onto the "boiseries," or carved wood paneling, by the "master-painters," as they were termed by their guilds. And finally, the coloring and filling-in were executed by the apprentices, the lowliest category in the guild hierarchy. But the craze for painted furniture was such that the demand greatly exceeded the supply; everyone who was anyone wanted furniture designed by the well-known artists. Accordingly, these gentlemen had their designs printed up by the thousands, and the printed designs could then be hand-colored by the humble apprentices, cut out, and glued onto furniture and panels in an infinite variety of decoupage designs. The master-painters' noses, of course, were out of joint at finding this relatively mass-produced and (to their prejudiced eyes) inferior "pasticherie" even more popular than their own work. So they coined the deprecatory epithet, "l'arte del povero." And the *découpeurs* themselves, keeping face, or *figura,* in true Italian style, adopted the term in a kind of nose-thumbing retaliation, and kept it as their own. We turn to 18th century England, and the *Ladies' Amusement Book,* published in 1762—a prime example of prints made solely for decoupage. It contains designs by so well-known an artist as Jean Pillement, who was famous as well for his enchanting chinoiserie.

England also produced Mrs. Delaney, whose cut flower miniatures are utterly fantastic. Comparable to the fabulous glass flowers at Harvard, hers, at the Victoria and Albert Museum in London, are a complete tour de force: you can look at them under a microscope and still be mystified by how they could possibly have been cut or glued.

At the court of Louis XVI and Marie Antoinette, decoupage became a hobby. The French queen and her court ladies blithely snipped up original Bouchers, Watteaus, Fragonards, Pillements—

anything they could lay their hands on, to make fans, boxes, table-tops, screens or whatever took their fancy.

After the dissolution of the guilds at the end of the 18th century, the art became virtually extinct. Sadly enough, decoupage (the art, that is; not the word, which simply means a cutting, or something cut out) is all but unknown in France today, except by a few connoisseurs and collectors of old Venetian furniture.

Certainly decoupage in various versions was practiced by many individuals in the 19th century: look at all the Victorian compositions of embossed valentines, magazine and newspaper cuttings and pinprickings; and the beautiful decoupage in the Biedermeier style, at which Miss Caroline Duer was a marvel in the 1940's.

3. *How I got involved.*

People constantly ask me when and where I learned decoupage. Well, it happened in 1928, when I had just started school in Switzerland, at "Le Rosey." My mother and I were invited to spend the Easter holidays with the family of a school chum of mine at their *manoir* (a kind of fortified manor house, half-castle, half-farm and manor) near St. Lô in Normandy.

Mother was collecting old Venetian furniture at the time, and I had been drawing and painting ever since I could first hold pencil or brush. Neither of us was prepared for what we found at St. Lô: the manoir was filled with beautiful painted and lacquered furniture, boiserie, screens, boxes, trays, bibelots of every sort . . . it was like a glowing jewel box filled with opals; it was as though the rooms were lit with sunlight from within.

Our delight and astonishment increased when we were told that the "painted" Venetian furniture was all covered with cut and colored paper, glued on and lacquered. Moreover, *it was all homemade,* we were told further; it had been a family hobby for generations. Our excitement really got out of hand, and our hosts were as excited as we were, we being the only people who had ever shown any real interest in this curious hobby. Their neighbors and friends affectionately considered them gently balmy people who cut out paper dolls—and couldn't have cared less. (Both the French and the English love, tolerate and value true eccentrics, whose American counterparts usually fare less well.)

And in the "library," an octagonal tower room, I discovered that the "books" that jammed the shelves from floor to ceiling were, in reality, named and numbered boxes filled with cuttings; roses, leaves, garlands, cupids—name it; it was there!

Our friends, it seems, were descendents of an old guild family, and when the guilds were disbanded at the time of the French Revolution, decoupage, as we've already seen, became a lost art. As far as they knew, they were the sole heirs to the tradition, which had become a family art, taught to each son and daughter who in turn passed on the old skill to their children.

They had retained all the original techniques and formulas for glue, protective varnish, etc., exactly as used in the 18th century. They offered to teach us all they knew, provided that we would agree to pass it on and not let it die. Mother, up to her ears as a grande couturiere, writer and columnist, demurred—but I jumped, and in view of tragic subsequent developments in history, it's lucky that I did. I don't think I ever spent happier days; I was like a piece of blotting paper, absorbing all that our Norman friends could teach me.

Then came World War II. Mother and I escaped with our skins, but our friends were less fortunate: St. Lô is now a French national monument of destruction. It was up to us to carry on the priceless heritage our friends had bequeathed to us.

I myself spent five years in the army, and when I returned to the United States, I found some of the formulas intact, but others had been partially lost. Mother and I, from memory, slowly and painstakingly reassembled them. Faithfully fulfilling the promise we had made to those who had taught us, we ourselves started to teach, so as to transmit to all of you this precious heritage of decoupage, adding to it the many new techniques and variations we evolved, adapted or discovered.

STYLES, ONCE OVER LIGHTLY

Let me speak my customary piece: this will be no erudite essay on European styles of the past four centuries. Tomes are available on this inexhaustible subject, and I want, as I do throughout this book, to focus on you, the practicing *découpeur,* and the prints you're likely to find yourself working with.

You may know much more on the subject than I'm going to tell you; if so, bear with me. Simply by way of guiding you through the maze of decoupage styles, many of which overlap in actuality, I'm giving you a loose listing of their general categories over the centuries. I'll clarify and illustrate as we go along.

3. *Table and slipper chair in the Louis XV manner. Chair decorated with French flowers in chinoiserie style, on Sèvres pink and celadon green ground. Table in Pillement figures; French flowers form the cartouche on Sèvres pink and pale Venetian blue. From Manning Studio by Mrs. William H. Sweet, Brookline, Mass.*

17th century: *baroque; classic; grotesque*

18th century: *rococo* or *rocaille; chinoiserie, singerie*

19th century: *Biedermeier; Milles Fleurs; Victorian; Trompe l'oeuil*

Why the emphasis on these three centuries? Fair question. They constitute the eras of engravings and etchings, and of the popularity of decorated furniture and bibelots. So remember that when we talk of "styles" of decoupage, we aren't referring to styles of furniture, but rather to those of the prints used (sometimes related, but not invariably) and also of the *manner* in which they are used in decoupage. Plate 3 offers an elegant example of coordinated furniture and decoupage style. The table and chair are, as indicated, in the Louis XV style, and the decoupage—French chinoiserie and Jean Pillement—are of the same rococo period. But a baroque print, for example, could easily emerge looking very Victorian—or very contemporary, depending on the taste and sense of design of the *découpeur* in each case.

Now to the styles themselves. *Baroque,* as we know it in architecture, painting and decoration, actually originated in Italy in the late 16th century, but reached the height of its overwhelming popularity throughout Europe in the 17th. Baroque can be described as the complex organization of rich plastic forms and rampant freedom of design; it marked the dethronement of, and reaction to, the classic, reaching its full richness during the reign of Louis XIV. It is curved, round, elaborate, ebullient and often tempestuous, with an opulent feeling of swirling movement: nothing is static. Is it similar to rococo? More on that later, but 17th century baroque, the source of some of our prints, is grand and florid, based on a concept of mass against light. That's essentially architectural terminology, and we can say that baroque is fuller, heavier, more architectural in its swirling strength than its direct descendant, rococo.

17th century classic is based, obviously, on Greek and Roman styles and motifs, but conceived in the lush style of the era, with

4. *A pair of 17th century figures illustrating the combination of classic and gro-*
tesque styles; Grisaille on ground of burnt apricot. Mrs. W. James Moore, Lowell,
Mass.

characteristically elaborate borders, garlands, wreaths and swags
(Plate 4).

My own definition of *grotesque* is a mad Hallowe'en party at-
tended by an assemblage of refugees from the classics. And a wild
ball it is, too: satyrs, Apollo with an ass's head, Medusa with her
celebrated reptilian coiffure, heads both animal and human
suspended from garlands, three-headed hydras—and other
couplings of the outrageous with the decorous, all based on the
classic Greek and Roman concept of tragi-comedy.

Plate 5 gives us a three-in-one example of style-blending, as
threatened, or promised, above. It shows us three baroque boxes,
using both grotesque and classic elements. You see that, used in
decoupage, grotesque can appear more "classic" than classic itself,
very prim and proper: it's making fun of itself and laughing at your
shocks. (Observe the grave-faced, centaur-like grotesque type
awaiting you at the bottom of the center box in Plate 6.) And

5. LEFT: *Rosewood desk box with baroque scrolls and birds.* CENTER: *Mahogany apple in grotesque.* RIGHT: *Walnut cigar box in baroque classic. Mrs. W. James Moore.*

6. LEFT: *Miniature knife box with decoupage of baroque and grotesque architectural ornaments, on chrome yellow ground.* CENTER: *Cigarette box in black and white grotesques. Lid carved, gilded, and inlaid with marbleized papers of lapis lazuli, malachite and rose quartz, with narrow gold braid banding.* RIGHT: *Bombe box with grotesque design on orange marbleized ground. Mrs. W. James Moore.*

7. *Antique English walnut knife box, circa 1790, inlaid with Circassian walnut with decoupage of baroque and grotesque engravings, giving the effect of Dutch marquetry under an infinite number of mache varnish coats. Mrs. W. James Moore.*

look at the walnut English knife-box (Plate 7), lavish with baroque swags, leaferie, garlands et al., and, just below the keyhole, the decapitated character suspended, in classic symmetry, from a charming bow arrangement.

I needn't tell you that grotesquerie, as an art concept, dates back to the very beginning and threads its way through all of art, as seen, for example, in the marvelous gargoyles and related grotesques found on the capitals of cloister columns in 13th and 14th century cathedrals . . . it's a permanent and pervading tradition; in decoupage it can be a delight. Enjoy it.

We referred to *rococo* (coined, it's said, from the combination of French *rocaille*, meaning rock work, and *coquille*, meaning shell) above. It superseded both baroque and classicism during the era of Louis XV. And, as you can see, it's an offshoot of baroque in its abandonment of rules, in its free asymmetrical handling of forms, and in its ornateness. But it's really less grandiose and more delicate, with a new lightness, delicacy and charm—a change from sobriety and heaviness. Its leitmotifs are shells and rocks

8. *Tole tray in full rococo style. Decoupage of typical scrolls, wheat sheaves and Boucher cupids.* Mrs. James Powers, Needham, Mass.

9. *Silver chest. Ground of silver tea paper. Baroque scrolls in deep yellow and greens; rococo flowers and figures in 18th Century Palette. Mrs. Frances D. Cross, Harvard, Mass.*

(hence its name), but ribbons, garlands, scrolls, cupids (see Plate 8) have their role too; curves and curlicues abound, and a straight line is the supreme sin. Plate 9 encompasses both baroque, in its rich, heavy scrollwork, and the more lyric rococo, seen on the lid of the box: the 18th century maid and gallant and the delicate traceries of the branches. Asymmetrical design carries the day, although at first glance a rococo print may appear symmetrical. However, if you look closely, you'll see that the two sides are actually totally different; it's the perfect balance that makes them seem alike. Plate 10, which is rococo chinoiserie, offers a prime example: panels left and right each have a bit of leaf-like ornamentation jutting out into space in identical positions, occupying

identical areas. Note, however, the difference in detail. This is the rococo world of unidentical equilibrium.

You recall that in our informal history, I cited Venice as the probable point of origin of European decoupage: Venice was where Italian rococo could be found in its most brilliantly decorative form.

Next, *chinoiserie,* the fantasy child of 18th century Europe. This is the rococo concept of the fabulous walled empire of Cathay, the land of the Celestial Empire whence came the fabled lacquers and porcelains so much in demand, as the techniques for creating both were still unknown in Europe at the start of the century. Meissen, Sèvres, and the European lacquers such as the famous *vernis martin* came later in the century.

In the European imagination, Kublai Kahn still reigned in Xanadu, over an empire of exotic folk clad in shimmering silks and fantastic hats, who sipped tea in porcelain pagodas with tinkling golden bells, and who were carried about in gorgeous sedan chairs across lacquered "moon" bridges.

Strictly fantasy; no European had really been inside China for centuries with the exception of a few privileged holders of trading concessions at specified ports, where they were barely permitted to land, there to trade with thirteen (no more, no less) merchants named by the Emperor, and then to depart as quickly as possible. Chinoiserie is the child of imagination and wishful thinking run riot. It's charming. See Plate 11 and 12. The prints of both Jean Pillement (Plate 13) and Boucher make delightful use of it.

Even more fantastic is *singerie,* the term deriving, of course, from the French *singe* or monkey. It depicts a world of monkeys fancifully dressed as mandarins, swinging from treetops of peacock feathers, or playing musical instruments in the powdered court

10. *Six-foot screen; chinoiserie decoupage of hand-colored Pillement figures, flowers and scrolls. Ground of brilliant celadon blue; decoupage in 18th Century Palette. Designed by Maybelle Manning; executed by Mrs. Everett L. Cuneo, Fort Lauderdale, Florida.*

11. One of a pair of wall panels, 28" x 45". Decoupage of chinoiserie, hand colored in 18th Century Palette on ground of Venetian green. Designed by Maybelle Manning; executed by Frances D. Cross.

12. Large octagonal box, 14" x 10". Decoupage of Pillement chinoiserie figures and scenes of "Games of Chinese Children at Play," with borders, toys, umbrellas etc. illuminated in thread-thin cut gold braid. Pompadour blue ground. By the Mannings. In author's collection. (See Plate 53 for inside of box.)

wigs of the then current mode, or waving banners and riding in lacquered palanquins. I wish I could produce a specimen, but must refer you, instead, to the charming *singerie* room at Sans Souci, created for Frederick the Great of Prussia. It's known as the "Voltairezimmer," because Voltaire presumably once occupied it as Frederick's guest. And there's an exquisite *chinoiserie-singerie*-paneled salon in the Château of Chantilly; and examples of Chinese Chippendale, quite a different manifestation of the same craze, abound.

13. Hexagon cigarette box. Pillement design of the "Five Senses of Nature." Visible on lid, the melon or "taste," and on box, the telescope or "sight." Center ground in gold leaf on gesso; ground of outside cartouche in Pompadour blue.

The style I've termed *Mille Fleurs* bridges the 18th and 19th centuries. Don't confuse it in a technical way with either the Gothic tapestries or the design known by the same name: in our free-for-all world of decoupage, *Mille Fleurs* refers to an all-over pattern of everything and anything: what better example than my grandmother's desk (Plate 14), which sports the most incredibly diverse décor, ranging from Cupids to Abraham Lincoln, George Washington, the White House a-building, an early foot-pedal Singer sewing machine, and the elegantly draped, centrally-placed legend, reading upside-down, "Presents for June 1937." Basic *Mille fleurs* technique: Cut everything you can find from prints, newspapers, catalogues, magazines et al., and strew over the entire surface of your piece. The design must, of course, have organization and even theme; note the rococo-like balance on the desk—but for the rest it's *sauve qui peut*, or each man for himself. With some kind of half-restraint in design, you can achieve an enchanting effect.

Now squarely in the 19th century, we encounter *Victorian* decoupage in full bloom; see the Victorian assemblages shown on Plate 15, complete with mother-of-pearl, butterflies and turtle-doves. Some, such as these, are enchanting (see also Plate 16); some of it is so atrocious that it's almost wonderful.

Another 19th century specialty is *Trompe l'oeuil* (literally "fool the eye." It's an art that creates an optical illusion: we see it in framed paintings; or on furniture, as in the case of a closed drawer painted so as to seem partly open, with a scarf or part of a necklace hanging out—only it isn't. This style can also be used in decoupage, but only with extremely realistic prints; shadows must be skillfully painted in so that the flat print seems to acquire an actual dimensional presence, as though you could pick it up.

14. An example of Milles Fleurs *design. Lady's desk, painted black, with decoupage of newspaper cuttings ranging from "Hamlet" in the center to you-name-it. Lavishly inlaid with mother-of-pearl. Designed and executed by the author's grandmother at the age of 96. (You see, there is still hope!)*

15. *Pair of Victorian decoupages in oval Biedermeier frames with bombe glass. Elevations of very early embossed flowers and mother-of-pearl butterflies on ground of yellow satin. Hiram Manning. In author's collection.*

(I once did a startling coffee table in *Trompe l'oeuil*: theater tickets and program, a glove, a bracelet, a burnt-out cigarette, an ashtray and a man's pocket-watch apparently tossed carelessly on the table after an evening at theater. All decoupage—except the watch, which was real, and which I set in, flush with the table's surface.) Experiment with this; it's a fascinating fun-form of decoupage.

The final school of 19th century print we'll deal with here is *Biedermeier*, essentially an Austrian form. The term was applied, detrimentally, to the imitative middle-class furniture of the epoch, by snobbish aristocrats who owned the far more elegant products of French Empire and Directoire style. ("Biedermeier" himself was

16. *Victorian chair and table. Decoupage of embossed valentine flowers, gold orna-ments and braid, lavishly inlaid with mother-of-pearl. Hiram Manning.* FRONT CEN-TER: *Biedermeier music box. Border of lid banded with mother-of-pearl. Decoupage of old valentine flowers and cupids. Maybelle Manning. In author's collection.*

not a furniture designer: he was "Papa Biedermeier," a humorous cartoon character who was also the subject of light verse in the *Fliegende Blätter,* a journal of the day.) Biedermeier-style decoupage could be mistaken for Victorian if it weren't for the rigidity of the design. It's basically flowers (most often embossed Valentine-like flowers) massed symmetrically to form a frame for another bouquet, or for cupids and doves, all matched to perfection: red rose left, red rose right, and so on, almost in the Byzantine manner of flower arranging. See Plates 16 (music box) and 17. As for the derided simple furniture, inlaid sparsely with black wood or white bone: it's worth a fortune today!

So much for styles of the past. To the little I've said, add all you can: read, and look. Libraries and museums abound with information and examples.

And as for today: we are no longer in an era of prints, etchings and lithography, but you'll find much at hand that may well suit your tastes and stimulate your *découpeur's* imagination.

17. Antique tole Venetian lavabo, redone on black ground in Bierdermeier style, with valentine flowers and gold braid, to hold collection of Second Empire French bead flowers. Hiram Manning. In author's collection.

Never forget that a "style," as such, is the current popular expression of the taste of a given period, superseded by others when people no longer want it. So it's you who possess the styles, not they you. Learn them until you are free of them, and can do with them as you wish.

A FEW WORDS ON DESIGN

These remarks will be informal, practical rather than theoretical, and I hope they'll relate entirely to your own work and experience as a practicing *découpeur* in action, and not to the art section of the library.

I'm often asked, "How do you design a piece of decoupage?" And I'm hard put to it to answer. And my answer may not be yours. We can say roughly that there are two ways of conceiving, and then executing, *any* work of art: first, you can start with a complete concept already formed in your mind's eye, and then set about actualizing it. Or, method No. 2, your imagination is triggered off by some isolated element—a color effect, a fragment of something, a picture or an object—that acts as a catalyst; it sets you into creative motion and you find yourself building a whole entity around it. (A writer, for example, may conceive of an entire plot, a developed idea—and then find the details he needs to give it life and substance. Or, instead, he may hear a fragment of conversation, overhear some curiously provocative bit of dialogue, and it forms the germ of an entire story, even of a novel.) To put it succinctly, from the general to the particular, or from the particular to the general.

I myself belong to the former school: the completed object pops up in my field of interior vision, and I then go about choosing prints and colors that recapture, as closely as possible, this pre-formed picture.

That's *my* way—and, granted, it may well be because I've been steeped in decoupage for so long that I'm what you might call "design-prone": my mind "sees" in terms of all-over design.

But this is cold comfort to the average beginner, who usually, although erroneously, thinks he hasn't the foggiest notion of how to create a design. Actually he's much closer to it than he realizes. Let me try to help you form and develop your own design ideas as you go along, just as I've done with pupils in my classes.

Let's start with the object: what's it to be? What do you want to decoupage? A box? Fine; select the box—and its size, shape and form will certainly influence where we go from here: we've already started designing; we know our *form.*

Next, choose a print—and (see "Choosing the Print") our selection is enormous. Here you are really on your own; your personal predilections are what count. You may opt for something classical, rococo, or Victorian; you may be intrigued with a cupid, flowers, birds, a shell or a bit of chinoiserie.

Let's say you've chosen a classical print, with a figure, or figures, as one of its components. Happy coincidence; it fits onto the box in question. Next, we search around for other prints from which we can excerpt elements that add to it—scrolls, urns, swags, wreaths, garlands, what-have-you. They may be in keeping with the classical style of your original choice—but remember, this is your creation, and part of the free-wheeling prerogative of the *découpeur* is style-mixing. You may put anything with anything, just as long as the elements complement one another.

And what's our criterion for this, at least in part? Here we stumble on another basic design principle: *scale.* The elements you choose must be in proportion with one another *and* with the box. The size of the original print, or prints, is irrelevant, because you'll be cutting everything apart. If the figures you've selected are standing on pedestals, and you find that proper scale demands that they be a bit taller, nothing's to stop you from cutting out bases from another print to build them up to the height you feel looks right. This is just what was done, for example, with Plate 18. Remember that you're forming *a new entity of your own;* I can't stress this point too much.

18. Sliding panels, 12" x 23", for a recessed wall cosmetic cabinet. Figure is Diana at her bath; pedestals, elevating figure, of black-and-white Piranesi 18th century prints. French flowers and foliage in soft greens, blues and pinks, with whimsical feather flowers in red and rose tones. Designed by Maybelle Manning; executed by Mrs. W. James Moore.

Next, *color*. Pick one of your favorites—for today at least. Blue, maybe? Fine; paint the box blue. And, having settled the ground, we come to our color palette for the prints. Now: bear in mind that you'll want to focus on *two dominant color areas*, and two only: your *basic background*, already settled, and the figure or figures you've selected as your *"central motif."* The rest of the decoupage should be in relatively quiet colors that harmonize with and enhance your basic scheme. So, having chosen blue for your ground, pick a second color for your central focus. Eliminate blue, unless you pick a strongly contrasting shade—and then add three, four or more colors that please YOU, and that coordinate well with your two basic tones. (See "The Palettes.") AND NOW

STICK WITH THEM, or you'll wind up with a Mexican fiesta. When you come to apply your running border, braid, or whatever kind of connecting sequence you've chosen, keep to one general color tone; you don't want a patchwork quilt.

Let's pause for a brief summary: the design guidelines we've run into thus far are three: form, scale, and color. The fourth is the all-important matter of the *central motif*, your design focal point—and we ran into *that* when you selected that classic figure or group of figures. Remember that it can be *anything,* or a combination of anything: a bunch of shells, a suspended grotesque head, or a butterfly; the only rule is that you keep to it as the central motif. To my way of thinking, this is the Golden Rule of decoupage design, and most of the others are subordinate to it and, in a sense, derive from it.

Which leads us to *placement,* or the disposition of your elements. Place that central motif on your box in the spot where, to your way of thinking, it seems to fit best and where it seems to belong. Trust your instinct: put it where it first struck your eye when you looked at it in conjunction with the box. Glue it on. (Don't panic; you can always switch it around later, see "Gluing.") Next, try out bits and pieces of your subordinate elements—scrolls, wreaths, a ladybug. Rule? Just this: they must lead your eye towards, and not away from, your central motif. And now for a primary *non-*rule: your central motif, despite our name for it, does *not* have to be in the center. If you have a symmetrical look in mind, put it there by all means. But it can go just as well in the upper left, or lower right corner, provided that you compensate for this asymmetry by *balance,* through the use of weight or color. (Take a look at the walnut cigar box on the right of Plate 5; do you see where the group of figures is placed? Lower left-hand corner. Makes them look in motion or flight, and the resultant effect is free and lovely.)

But whether your effect be symmetrical or not, the central focus must never be lost. Everything you add must direct the eye, as if

19. *Pair of cachepots with decoupage of Pillement chinoiserie figures, and (CEN-TER) gold-footed box, decoupaged in tones of lavender and terra cotta—showing uses of florals, butterflies etc. as central motifs. Mrs. Charles Arnold, Andover, Mass. and Mrs. James Powers, Needham, Mass., respectively.*

20. *Relatively sparse design on tin pitcher creates contemporary effect through use of space. Design of mushrooms, grasses etc. on Venetian flame ground. Gold-footed box with gold-leaf ground uses design of Boucher cupids and 18th century Persian flowers in Grisaille. Both designed and executed by Mrs. J. Verser Conner.*

it were on a trolley-track, toward your dominant element. This track, or network of tracks, may be straight or curlicued, closed or open, continuous or broken; they may be composed of ferns, feathers or flying fish just as long as they guide your eye, as the crow flies, to the focus of your design.

Finally, don't forget that open space is just as much a part of your design as the cuttings you apply. Awareness of this *relationship between used and unused space* constitutes the sixth component of this highly informal, discover-as-you-go foray into the field of decoupage design. A particularly apt illustration of the use of space is Plate 20: On the tin pitcher, the branches, mushrooms and butterfly are placed on an essentially open ground in a highly effective manner that's at once oriental and contemporary in its sparse juxtapositions. Even in an all-over pattern such as *Milles Fleurs,* what's left uncovered is as important as the cut-out elements. (What's a better example of this principle than lace? No holes, no lace.)

To sum up, then, from our design-as-you-go procedure: 1. Shape or form, i.e., your surface. 2. Scale, or proportion. 3. Color and color relationships. 4. Focus, or central motif. 5. Placement, or balance. 6. The use of space.

The best piece of advice I can give you (and the most difficult to follow) is this: Know when you're through and then QUIT. Discipline yourself, or you'll wreck your entire concept. If you've got one more cherished snippet left over, use it on the next decoupage—or else live dangerously; throw it away.

A last and fundamental injunction: Look at, and study, beautiful art works in any form. Paintings, sculpture, tapestries; anything that delights your eye. Remembering what we've said, try to unravel and identify the threads that lead to the central motif. When you begin to understand why your eye travels there, inevitably, you'll be able to think in similar terms as you design your own decoupages. Design is a creative, visual thing, not a set of rules, so train your eye; how did the artist make you see it that way?

Grasp just this, and you'll have clear sailing—and a beautifully designed blue decoupaged box to boot. Your eye will flow over and around the box, seeing it, not as a random assortment of polychromed, glued-on cuttings, but as a rhythmic and integrated whole.

And now, shall we begin?

2 CHOOSING THE PRINT

VALUABLE OLD PRINTS

First of all, let me make one thing clear to every reader of this book, to every *découpeur* and *découpeuse*, to every collector of fine prints, and to every head of a museum: I totally and completely disapprove of, and will have nothing to do with, the cutting up of valuable old prints. I never have and I never intend to. Many a pupil has brought fine, valuable, old prints to me to be cut up and has been given short shrift. I tell him to frame it, keep it, or sell it.

On the other hand, there are many (not too many) old prints of no particular value floating about with torn corners, watermarks, etc., that may be cut up for, say, a *vue d'optique*. Those I will use, as they are of no value to a collector. But that is as far as I will go. I am a collector of fine old prints, and I value and love them. I have seen many such prints cut up when the reproduction would have done as well—in fact, even better. Sometimes, when valuable old prints are brought to me already cut, I have no choice except to preserve them in decoupage; but I make my disapproval clear and the incident is seldom repeated.

In rare bookshops and print shops and at a rare price, too, one can find books of 17th- and 18-century prints cut and colored in those centuries for decoupage. Those I will use and gladly. It is what they were meant for; it takes them out of their shut pages and brings them to life again, and thus they fulfill their "kismet," or fate.

For decoupage, I personally prefer to collect old prints, and have them reproduced on a copper plate, using special inks on special water bond paper, to resemble exactly the original (which I

21. *Seven color-print covers of Hor-*
ticultural Magazine *were the source*
of this decoupage of papayas, on a
ground of Chinese apricot, which
decorates this large Chippendale
coffee-table tray. Maybelle Man-
ning. In author's collection.

keep in portfolios or in frames.) These black-and-white prints I
reproduce in lots of five hundred or a thousand. They can then be
hand colored by oil-pencil. (Do you recall my account of the
origin of "l'arte del povero"? This is the same procedure!) These
are the prints my pupils use, with a choice of some several thousand.
I have them in a catalogue too. But I reproduce from *originals*
only, *never* from copies. Such reproductions become muddy and
fuzzy. There are a great many of them, reproductions of reproductions, and I refuse to use them, nor do I allow my pupils to
do so. Too much work is involved to start off with a fuzzy print
on heavy slick paper. And we are trying to pursue decoupage
or *scriban* as something that you can, if you have the talent, turn
into an *art*.

OTHER PRINTS

As to other prints . . . anything is grist for your mill, provided that
you choose carefully. Colored prints will never have the same
effect under varnish as a hand-colored one done with oil pencils,
but they *are* perfectly beautiful under glass or in a *vue d'optique*.
Somehow they become shopworn and faded under varnish. But in
buying a colored print, look at it carefully. Are the colors *true?*
Is it vaguely fuzzy? Are you not quite satisfied with it? Then don't

buy or use it, for it will look no better under glass than it does in the printshop, and under varnish it will look even worse.

Some colored prints, while perfectly beautiful and beautifully printed, but certainly not originally intended for decoupage, will turn every color of the rainbow when sealer is applied, or else the colors will run and bleed. This will certainly upset you, but not half as much as it would *after* they were cut, glued, and part of your

22. *Piranesi architectural prints (18th century) and classic figures in Grisaille were the print choices for this wall hanging set in an early 19th century burl maple frame. Mrs. W. James Moore.*

design. So, *seal any colored print first to test it*. If it works, fine! If it does not, chalk it up to experience.

Prints from magazines, books, etc., with print or another picture on the back can be used if, when the sealer is applied, the print or color on the reverse side does not show through.

Any and all prints may be used in decoupage IF, after sealing, they appear all right to you.

Thinning the Print

Prints on heavy or thick paper can be used in a *vue d'optique* and under varnish, but will require dozens of additional coats. These prints can be peeled, and thus made thinner. Moisten the back of the print with white vinegar, but don't soak it. Let it sit a minute or so, and with your finger or a damp, well-wrung-out sponge, rub the paper off until it is as thin as you want it. Wipe it clean and remove the vinegar with a clean, damp sponge. This won't work all the time, but 90 percent of the time it will. Let the print dry, seal it, and then you may use it.

Hand-colored prints and precolored prints may be used together in a decoupage provided they are visually compatible, which is usually not the case. But then, *you* must be the judge of that.

Photostats, photographs, Xerox reproductions, etc., while marvelous in themselves, cannot be used in decoupage under varnish. A photograph or photostat has a prepared surface to "take" the photo. Firstly, it wants to curl up; secondly, it will not take the proper color; and thirdly, in time it fades and the color with it. Oh, yes! You can glue it down and varnish it, but it won't stay permanently.

Xerox and other similar machine reproductions come out beautifully, but the moment the sealer touches them, the surface turns bright yellow and the print, coloring and all, comes off like scuffed-up cellophane, and you are left with a piece of blank paper. This holds true for *every* machine for reproducing prints

23 and 24. Folded paper cutting. The kind you did in kindergarten, slightly elaborated. Designs for wallpaper by the Mannings. (See Plate 78.)

that comes on the market. I test them all, and believe me, when I find the one that works for decoupage, I'll mortgage my house, "Missie" my dog, and myself, and buy it! Meanwhile, I'll stick to fine reproductions of fine old prints, printed from a copper plate and hand-colored in the old way. Or I'll make my own!

Remember that your decoupage or *scriban* is not one whit better than the print or prints used to compose it. However trite and banal it sounds, it is still true that "you can't make a silk purse out of a sow's ear."

By the way, folded paper cuttings are perfect for decoupage and allow a wonderful freedom in planning your design for any period, or for a creation with a contemporary flair that expresses exactly how you feel at a given moment. Two sophisticated examples are shown in Plates 23 and 24. A simpler completed piece is shown in the lamp section (Plate 77).

3 PREPARING THE SURFACE FOR DECOUPAGE

PREPARING OLD WOOD

If the wood has previously been finished, the old finish must be removed. Any good paint and varnish remover will do; just follow the manufacturer's instructions on its use. Then sand the wood smooth and proceed as for new wood.

25. Nest of tables in progress. Completed table shows decoupage with cartouche border of baroque scrolls in golden tones, and motifs of Pillement chinoiserie figures in 18th Century Palette. Ground is of pale Venetian blue; borders are Venetian blue with corner cartouches of deep lapis lazuli. Mrs. James Powers.

26. Tole cocktail tray. Two-toned ground of black jade and Chinese apricot. Cupids in Sanguine Palette, morning glories in blue. Gold braid used in border of center cartouche, center of trellis, stars on pierced gallery, cartouches and birds. Mrs. Kimball Powning, Wayland, Mass.

PREPARING NEW WOOD

1. Seal the object with protective sealer (see page 77) inside and out. Use it generously and let it soak in. Leave yourself one dry surface to hold it by or set it on, or you will have sticky hands and a smudgy surface. When it is dry (ten to fifteen minutes or longer, depending on the weather), seal the last remaining surface and let it dry.

2. Paint all surfaces of it with one, two, or sometimes three coats of decoupage paint (see Sources of Supply) applied sparingly and well brushed out (and no drips, please). Allow each coat to dry overnight before applying a second coat. Two coats are usually sufficient if properly applied.

3. When the object is painted to your satisfaction, apply another coat of protective sealer. Apply it sparingly this time, and brush it out in all directions until the brush begins to "drag" or

27. *Large cachepot, 12″ x 12″, custom-made of zinc. Decoupage of 18th century "Garden Fantasy" prints. Hand-colored in 18th Century Palette on ground of Venetian yellow. Maybelle and Hiram Manning. In author's collection.*

lightly "pull." Then apply to adjoining area, overlapping your brush strokes. Do not attempt to apply it to the whole surface at once; you will flood it and get into a sticky mess. Do about a three-inch square area at a time. When it is dry, it is ready to be decoupaged.

PREPARING METAL: TIN, TOLE, ETC. (ANY METAL THAT IS SUBJECT TO RUST)

1. If this is an old piece, remove the old finish with any good paint and varnish remover, following the directions for that particular

product. Even if the object is new and painted black (or sprayed) that does not mean it has necessarily been rust-proofed, and the original finish should be removed. Take my advice; on one occasion I did not remove it—and I regretted it.

2. When the old finish has been completely removed, apply Rusticide or any good rust remover available at art supply or paint stores. Then scrub with fine steel wool #0000 until all rust spots have been removed.

3. Scrub the object with any good scouring powder, just as you would a pot or pan, and dry.

4. Paint it with plain denatured alcohol or shellac thinner. Allow this to evaporate for a minute or two and do not touch it with your bare hands, because wherever your hand has touched it, rust will eventually form from the natural salts on your skin (like finger marks on silver as it tarnishes). If you must touch or move it, use gloves, cotton, a clean cloth, tissue paper, paper towels, etc.

5. Take a good red metal sanding primer or rust-inhibiting paint (available at any good paint store; it is like the red paint used for painting fire escapes and bridges; it stops rust. Thin it by adding one-third gum turpentine to two-thirds metal sanding primer, and apply three thin coats, one coat a day.

6. When the last coat is dry, sand very lightly, just enough to remove any dust bumps or gritty feeling.

28. *Three wall switches decoupaged on metal in 18th Century Palette on Venetian yellow and ivory grounds; the second piece of decoupage ever given me. Designed and executed by Mrs. J. Verser Connor.*

7. Apply a thin, well-brushed-out coat of protective sealer. Let dry.

8. When dry, apply as many coats of paint as are necessary (two thin coats are better than one thick coat).

9. Seal again with protective sealer and you are now ready to decoupage it.

This process may seem to resemble the labors of Hercules, but it really only takes ten minutes here, five there each day, and it's done! Also, it is worth the effort because it will effectively eliminate rusting. If you skip this process, you are chancing having your completed decoupage, which may represent months of work, ruined a year or two later when rust spots suddenly appear. Your only choice then will be to live with the rust spots, or to strip it and start over.

PREPARING OTHER SURFACES

Decoupage can be applied to any natural surface: wood, driftwood, tin, tole, steel, iron, lead, silver, stone, porcelain, pottery, slate, marble, glass, but, I regret to say, it will *not* work with plastic.

Any surface you plan to use must be cleaned first: dusted, shined or washed. (Silver, alas, no matter how well it is polished, will tarnish in time, but can still be very beautiful, if you like that effect— many do.)

To decoupage any cleaned surface other than one to be used under glass, first, apply a coat of protective sealer. Then use that surface as your ground, or paint it, if you wish. If you paint it, you will again have to seal the paint with protective sealer before decoupaging it. Decoupage *over* glass is sealed first. Decoupage *under* glass is not sealed first. You will find complete directions for decoupage under glass (lamps, etc.), later.

4 COLOR PALETTES FOR DECOUPAGE

Here I list all the colors you will ever need; later in this section I divide them according to the palettes in which they are used, should you prefer to buy the pencils only as you require them. Usually I use Prismacolor pencils, but for certain colors I will specify Derwent English pencils or Colorama pencils. The colors are listed roughly by their families. And remember, color your print and seal it before you cut it out.

MATERIALS

Hard gum eraser
A good pencil sharpener
Smooth cardboard or a pad to work on. (Don't use glass, it is too hard and will cause your coloring to look scratchy.)
Colored pencils:
    black; white; slate gray.
    lemon yellow; gold; sand; yellow orange; orange yellow; ochre; terra cotta; dark brown.

29. *This is what you start with. A black and white print, uncolored.*

30. *The finished piece of cutting, colored, sealed, and cut all in one piece; you whack it up later as you design.*

31. *Large knife box, after an 18th century model. Grisaille Palette on jet black ground. Print by Raphael, who reproduced it and others from his own designs for the Loggia of the Vatican Library. Frances D. Cross.*

32. *Decoupage in black and white, using the Grisaille Palette, gives this antique mahogany tea caddy the effect, under varnish, of Dutch marquetry. Designed by Maybelle Manning; executed by Mrs. Clara Friedman, Brookline, Mass.*

flesh; light flesh; scarlet lake; Colorama madder red; Derwent no. 14 and no. 22 (magenta-ish, wild and wonderful); Derwent no. 65 burnt carmine (to use with or instead of black).

ultramarine blue; true blue; sky blue; indigo blue.

violet; light violet; lavender; cerise.

pink (a stinky pink, strawberries-and-cream); blush pink (to use only under glass).

grass green; peacock green; eve green; Paris green; apple green; green bice (to use under glass).

THE PALETTES

These are traditional palettes, but of course you may vary them to your heart's content *after* you have learned your basic techniques; they help you from getting confused with too many colors at the start.

Grisaille Palette

You will need pencils in the following colors: black; white; slate gray.

Once you master the Grisaille Palette, you will know the basics of using your pencils and will not be confused by color, which cannot mask your errors.

The name comes from the French word for gray, which is *gris*. It is pronounced like "greeze eye." My pupils and I affectionately call it the "grizzly palette" and let it go at that.

With the three pencils—black, white, and gray—you actually have a combination of five shades: black-white-gray; black-white; white-black; gray-white; white-gray.

The shade depends on which color you put on first. If you put black on first and then white, you get a gray, but not the same gray as the gray pencil would give you. Put white on first and shadow it with black, and you get white shaded into deep gray, and so on. Try them out on a piece of blank paper first, before you tackle your black-and-white print.

As an example, let's say you are coloring a Boucher cupid with clouds and ribbons. Use the three pencils in the order in which I name them; if you don't, you will get all mixed up on your first attempt.

For the cupid figures only, use, in the order listed:

black—for the deepest shadows of the body
slate gray—for the medium shadows
white—for highlights and to blend the black and gray with
black—(again) to accent some of the deeper shadows and for the eyes, eyebrows, lips, ears, etc.

For the cupid hair (and wings, if present), use:

white—all over
black—accent in quick light strokes with a sharp, sharp black pencil; don't *draw* the hair, *sketch* it in using quick hairlike strokes

For cupid ribbons and/or drapery, use:

black—in shadows
white—all over
black—(again) to reaccent with

For clouds, use:

gray—in shadowed parts
white—all over, heavy
gray—(again) to reaccent with

Sanguine Palette

You will need pencils in the following colors: scarlet lake; dark brown; terra cotta; madder red (Colorama); white; black (optional).

Sanguine, from the French word for blood, *sang*, literally means the color of dried blood. "Song geen" is the nearest I can get to it phonetically. It is an extremely beautiful color used on a soft gray or gray-blue background, and is a perennial favorite with artists for sketching and finished drawings.

Try out any and every combination of the four colors with white on blank paper to get familiar with the various shades you can achieve, so that you know what you are after when you take your print to color. If you decide to add black here and there, be *very* chary of it, using it as an accent only! Remember, white is your blender and your highlight.

For clarification, let's color another cupid using the Sanguine Palette. Remember, these examples are only for explaining the color combinations and are *not* to be taken as my substitutions for your own personal taste. You choose your own colors as you choose everything else!

For the cupid figures only, use, in the order listed:

dark brown—for deepest shadows of body
terra cotta—for medium shadows
madder red—for lighter shadows
white—for highlights and to blend
terra cotta or madder red—(again) to accent some of the deepest shadows,
    and madder red (again) OR black for eyes, eyebrows, etc.

For the cupid hair (and wings, if present), use:

white—all over
madder red—accent in quick light strokes with a sharp pencil; don't draw
    the hair, sketch it using quick hairlike strokes.

For cupid ribbons and/or drapery, use:

scarlet lake—in shadows
white—all over
scarlet lake—(again) to reaccent

For clouds, use:

scarlet lake or madder red—in deepest shadowed parts
white—all over, heavy
scarlet lake or madder red—(again) to reaccent

Toile de Jouy Palette

We use the term "toile de Jouy" to mean a design adopted from
fabric and printed in one color on a cream or white background.
Landscapes, figures and florals are characteristic jouy prints.

You have your choice here of a red, a blue, or a green, or a combination of any one of them with blue and/or yellow as accents.
It is basically a monochrome palette with the exception of the Combination Palette (see below).

Again, you use the same technique as you did for the Grisaille
Palette (except for the Combination Toile Palette described
below).

For a Red Toile: burnt carmine (Derwent no. 61) ; scarlet lake; madder red (Colorama) ; white.

For a Blue Toile: indigo blue; ultamarine blue; true blue and/or sky blue; white.

For a Green Toile: grass green; peacock green; eve and/or Paris green; lemon yellow; white; black (optional)

These are the traditional colors, but if you wish to go off on your own, and of course you may, use any color you wish. You must, though, keep to a monochrome color. For example: violet, light violet, lavender, pink; white or dark brown; terra cotta, sand-flesh-white. Black may be added to any palette as a deep accent if you so desire, but take my advice and *only* add it at the very last—or you will end up with *very* muddy colors.

For a Combination Toile: Any one of the above with the addition of a yellow or blue as accents only, keeping them clear and not blended with the other colors. However, with the Red Toile, if you were coloring a scene with figures, you might do some of the figures in yellow or blue and keep the rest all red—trees, grass, flowers and all. Yellow additions: sand; yellow ochre; lemon yellow. Blue additions: ultramarine blue; indigo blue.

Chinoiserie or Pillement Palette

The Pillement Palette is rather like a peacock series of colors. You can use black and/or burnt carmine (Derwent no. 61) ; white madder red (Colorama) ; scarlet lake; pink; lemon yellow; orange; indigo blue; ultramarine; violet; grass green; peacock green.

The technique for its use is discussed under "Juxtaposing Colors" in *Coloring Techniques* where I explain the use of your pencils and how to combine colors.

Eighteenth Century or Full Palette

The Eighteenth Century or Full Palette is the full and enchanting gamut of colors, so you may use any combination you wish. But plan a general color scheme so that your colors will harmonize and complement each other. Included here is the shot silk or "changeable" taffeta look. The technique for getting this iridescent effect is described later (see Index).

33. *Prints in the Grisaille Palette, used on black jade ground outside and on Venetian flame ground inside, decorate this lidded wastebasket; the cupids are excellent examples of contour hand-coloring (see p. 69). Mrs. J. Verser Conner.*

5 COLORING TECHNIQUES FOR PRINTS

USING YOUR PENCILS

There are four basic ways to use your pencils:

1. Soft and shadowing with little or no pressure
2. Quick and nervous in short, inspirational strokes
3. Quick, firm accents, again nervously applied
4. By juxtaposition of colors

Whatever method you use, remember that you must keep your pencils *sharp!* Even with experienced pupils of many years stand-

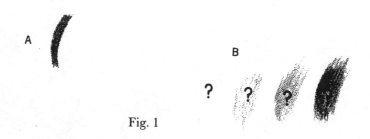

Fig. 1

ing, I have to keep reminding them of that fact, constantly and daily. Never press hard with your pencil to get a deep color, as in 1A. Use your pencil lightly, and go over the part you are coloring until you achieve the depth you want. The section you are working on must never be obliterated by color, or your print will wind up looking like a first kindergarten attempt. Add your colors as in **B** to achieve depth.

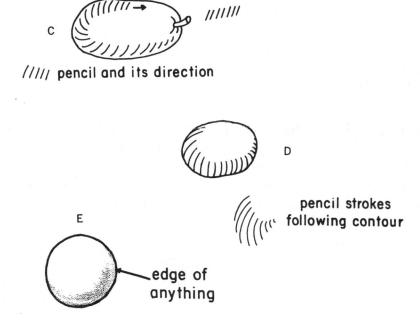

///// pencil and its direction

pencil strokes
following contour

edge of
anything

FOLLOWING THE CONTOURS

Follow the contour of what you are coloring. I don't mean the
grain of the print, but the contour of the detail you are working on.
If it is a cupid's tummy, color it round; if a pine tree, color it
pointed. If you are coloring a melon, say, color it as in C. Don't
run your pencil around and around the melon. Use it thus (D),
still following its contours. This is a coarse version, but the effect
I want you to get is shown in E.

This applies to the edge of anything you want to make round
or give depth to: ball, melon, column, arm, leg, tummy, tree trunk.
You go from deep at the edge to feather-nothing as it fades away
from the edge toward the center. This gives any part of your print

a roundness. To achieve various tones without sacrificing the round-ness of the arm, leg or tree trunk you are coloring, go from the inside of the shadowed-out edge and blend back into it, toward the outer or original edge already colored. You may use a lighter tone of that color or a totally different one.

COLORING A FLOWER

You're coloring a bluish, pinkish flower with a yellow center. From your pencils, pick two shades of blue, one dark, one light (ultra-marine and true blue, for example), plus pink, lemon yellow, and, as in *any* coloring *always,* black and white. *Never* forget your white. It is the most important pencil you own, acting as your blender. It is what water is to watercolor or turpentine is to oil color.

Place the ultramarine on the flower as shown in Figure 2. Then use your pink pencil, blending from the edge of the blue out onto each petal and from the tip back, in the same way that you applied the blue. Blend it partly back into the blue and out onto the white (or still uncolored) part. Never obliterate all your white, as it is your highlight; if you do, your print will go flat and dead.

Your flower should now look something like Figure 3. Plop some lemon yellow in the center and then, petal by petal, following the contour or shape of each petal, blend with your white pencil,

Fig. 2

Fig. 3

Fig. 4

going over the white or uncolored part. Don't be Dorothy Dainty; blend it firmly. Now your flower looks like Figure 4. It should be rounded, with shape and form, and the tones of pink and blue all softly blended so that you are not conscious of where or how they begin or end.

Now, take your black pencil (*sharp*) and accent around the center of the flower (accent with your original blues first). Use quick, light strokes of the black. And there you are, I hope, with a crisp, fresh-looking flower.

The exact method of applying the black is to sketch lightly in hair strokes around the center, then dab the tips. You may substitute or add burnt carmine for this effect.

Don't bear down all over and, just because you want a blue flower, smear the whole thing blue from stem to stern. It will wind up looking as if it were whacked out of blue paper, which you could have done in the first place as a donation to the children's nursery school halloween party. The basic idea to get firmly implanted in your mind is that you are dealing with black-and-white prints, etchings, or engravings that already have their own shadows and nuances. You are attempting to color them, not to obliterate them with color.

JUXTAPOSING COLORS

The most eye-deceiving juxtaposition of colors is the pointillism technique used by Seurat, the French Impressionist painter. He applied dots or strokes of color to a surface with such density that, seen from a distance, the dots or strokes seem to blend together to form a luminous whole.

In decoupage coloring, place the colors next to each other and *barely* blend them together (which Seurat did *not* do), Figure 5. Then blend them thoroughly with white, firmly applied, Figure 6. Reapply one or both colors and accent with them again. You can use three, four, or five colors this way in the Chinoiserie or Pille-

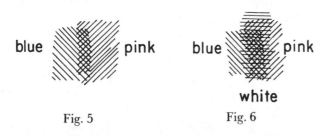

Fig. 5   Fig. 6

ment Palette to achieve peacock colors, or two or more in the Pillement and Eighteenth Century Palette to achieve a shot silk or iridescent look.

Let's take a "peacock" color. This would usually be for the Pillement Palette, but may be used in almost any palette, depending on your personal taste. Who's to argue? I believe that art should be free, and that anything may be put with anything else if you have the taste and the know-how to do it. For the "peacock" apply your basic colors from the outside in. (I will get you to the center, and back to the outside again afterwards.) Work from the outside into the center in this order:

1. Violet at the tips of flowers, edges of anything, beginnings of folds of drapery, etc.
2. Grass green juxtaposed and slightly overlapping back into the violet and projecting lightly onto uncolored area inward, shadowed.
3. Pink, the same, but don't obliterate your white.

Now work from the center back to the outside where you started, in this order:

1. Lemon yellow for the dead center.
2. Orange and/or peacock green, each juxtaposed and slightly blended, but again not obliterating the white or uncolored part where the outside and the inside join; leave a bit of no-man's-land of plain uncovered white.

Now take your white pencil and, with a good firm pressure, literally smear the colors together, from the outside in and from the inside out, also going over no-man's-land. Don't rub so hard that you turn the whole thing into a slick surface of white pencil, like a skating rink, but rub hard enough to blend and merge the colors. As I have said previously, what you are after is a blending of your various colors so that you are not conscious of where one color begins and the other starts and ends.

Then take your original color for the outside (in this case, violet) and "nervously" accent the edges, pulling and feathering inward from the edge. Reaccent your center, and then, if you wish, accent with either black or burnt carmine.

SHOT SILK LOOK

For a shot silk look, which applies mainly to robes, dresses, draperies, etc., you usually use two colors, or maybe three, always including white, of course. There are a number of possible combinations. In the examples I give, the first color is for the edges or deep shadows, and the second for medium shadows. The third (and fourth or fifth) is for highlight and accent. Barely "flick" on the accent color or colors here and there, as if a hummingbird or swallow of that particular color had darted over it. Before the last accent color is applied, use your white, all over, and reaccent with your first color. *Then* let the swallow dart, and not before.

Now here are a few basic combinations of colors for a shot silk look. (You can vary these and others in many ways, so try, experiment; you might end up with something good. I hope you will!) Apply, in the order named:

1. Violet, pink, white; accent with violet, flick with yellow.
2. Pink, white to blend, pink to accent, lemon yellow and apple green flicked.
3. Madder red, ultramarine blue, white to blend; ultramarine *or* madder red for accent; yellow, green, or pink to flick.
4. Black shaded out into gray (not gray pencil, but black shaded out), then lemon yellow to give you a green (if you apply the yellow first, you'll just get a shaded yellow).

These combinations are just basic. Experiment with others; many colors change when applied over another.

COLORING FOR DECOUPAGE UNDER VARNISH

There are two basic concepts of coloring for decoupage: under varnish and under glass. First, for under varnish, color me loud! If you have noticed the colors I have given you for various palettes for under varnish, most of the colors are bold, brilliant. There is a simple reason. The varnish tones, soften, subdues, and almost "tames" the colors. So for under varnish you want your colors louder, more brilliant, than you would normally use them, with contrast exaggerated. I don't mean heavier, I mean brighter. Make them like a fiesta or a carnival, because if you don't, after many coats of varnish they look like an old beige artificial-silk stocking.

The best tip I can give you in coloring for under varnish is to get yourself a piece of glass (about four by six inches), give it twenty coats of varnish and, as you color your print, place it over the print from time to time to get an idea of your ultimate result. It will give you quite a shock—so color that pale wan rose bright pink and that wasted-out, no-color blue bright blue. Place your varnished glass over it again until it is the color you want. By the time you've finished coloring your print this way, it will probably resemble Mardi Gras, but it will look attractive and hold its color under varnish. Or were you planning to frame it? In that case, we get to coloring for under glass.

34. Note the glass in frame at bottom left: it has twenty coats of varnish on it. The author, seen here coloring a print, will place the glass over it from time to time as he colors so as to get a vivid approximation of the final result (see p. 74).

COLORING FOR DECOUPAGE UNDER GLASS

For under glass you may use any colored pencil you wish: pale, wan, pastel, washed-out, whatever your heart desires, because there is no varnish to contend with. The technique for using your pencils remains the same, as do your palettes, but you may use the paler versions because under glass they are not going to change one iota. But once again, do not forget to leave some white and to blend with your white pencil.

COLORING FLESH TONES

For Greek figures, cupids, and flesh tones in general (barring a one-toned palette like Grisaille), I use these colors, in the order given, following the technique for the Grisaille Palette:
1. Dark brown for the edges
2. Terra cotta, blending inward
3. Pink, blending inward
4. Flesh, blending inward
5. Light flesh, blending inward, but never obliterating or covering up all the white or uncolored part
6. White, blending all over, following contours of object
7. Terra cotta to reaccent
8. Black, "nervously" sketched for eyebrows, eyes, etc.

SEALING AFTER COLORING

After your print is colored to your satisfaction and before you even begin to think of cutting it, seal it (see technique given under Protective Sealer). You will instantly see why I stressed white and highlights; they pop right up and your print suddenly glows. Allow it to dry ten to fifteen minutes, and it is ready to cut.

At any time, but *before* you seal your print, if your coloring does not please you, or if it has gone muddy, use the eraser. It will all come off and you may start over. So many beginners are timid about color until they find that they can erase it. So—use it!

35. *This small table has an antiqued gold border of hand-colored French flower scrolls by St. Non, to match its carved pedestal. This print has been sealed after coloring and before cutting. The scrolls are in greens, blues and pinks; the Boucher cupids in pale Sanguine Palette. The Mannings. In author's collection.*

6 PROTECTIVE SEALER

Protective sealer (see Sources of Supply) is not a finish in itself. It does precisely what its name promises: protects and seals. It is used under and over practically everything, up to the point of varnishing, then it bows out.

There are many sealers or fixatives on the market; charcoal fixative, pastel fixative, watercolor fixative, and a lot of other products that are being used in decoupage as sealers. Use them if you like, but they may go sour on you and not work. I cannot recommend them because I do not have the laboratory facilities for testing them all. I can, in honesty, only tell you what, after decades of experience, I know to work. What is so hard to explain to an amateur is that each product must bond or ally with the other. The sealer must ally with the wood and the paint, the sealed paint with the glue, and all of them with the varnish. If they don't, something—sealer, paint, glue, or varnish—will give way in time and your decoupage will fall apart. For the prime tragic example, take Leonardo da Vinci's *Last Supper*. He used oil paint on a plaster ground and it has all but flaked away. The two just did not bond or ally.

Whatever sealer you choose to use, *don't use shellac*. It is a marvelous product, but successive coats of varnish just will not adhere to it permanently. It contains its own natural wax and, chemically, varnish over wax will not work. It's like oil and water: both are fine, but not together.

Below I tell you how and when, and when *not*, to apply protective sealer.

WHAT TO SEAL

1. Raw wood: Apply sealer generously. Just let it soak in and seal. Don't worry about brushstrokes or bubbles, as they will all soak in and disappear.

2. Hand-colored prints: After the print is colored, but before cutting it, brush a coat of protective sealer on the front side, laying it on in one direction only. Don't brush back and forth or your colors may run. Blot it dry immediately with a crumpled paper towel, napkin or tissue. Do a small area at a time, a three-inch square for example, then proceed to the next area until the whole piece is sealed. Allow to dry ten to fifteen minutes. It is then ready to cut. The sealer will protect the paper from varnish discoloration; it will make cutting easier by giving the paper more body; and it will provide a coating that keeps the paper from getting mushy during the gluing and cleaning-off process.

Precolored prints: Test them first (see below) to be sure they are colorfast; then apply sealer as for hand-colored print.

3. On all painted surfaces and glued dry decoupage (after glue is cleaned off): Apply a thin, well-brushed-out coat of protective sealer. Brush it in all directions—east, west, north, south; not just back and forth in a straight line. Brush it lightly; sort of "fan" it with your brush, lightly touching it until the brush begins to drag or lightly pull and the protective sealer is no longer liquid or moving.

4. Over water gilt: Apply as for No. 3 above.

5. Never *under* water gilt: Sealer cannot be used on a gesso ground which you plan to water gild and/or burnish. The red burnishing clay just will not adhere.

6. Under oil gilt: Apply as on No. 3 above. But never *over* oil gilt—it will curdle everything and make it look like badly applied radiator paint.

TESTING PRECOLORED PRINTS FOR COLOR FASTNESS

Colored magazine or book prints, wallpaper or precolored prints of any kind should be tested for color by applying protective sealer to the front side and blotting dry with a crumpled paper napkin or tissue before attempting to cut it out or use it. If the print comes through from the back, it cannot be used. If it doesn't, then it is all right to use.

Some colors run horribly, depending on the inks used. Some colors change pleasantly, and, if you like the new color, use it. Again, this is trial and error. Test them first or you may find that a nice green leaf and a pink rose have turned magenta and purple *after* you have cut and glued them on. If the precolored print passes your test, proceed to apply protective sealer as directed above.

THINNING DOWN THE SEALER

The thinner for protective sealer is denatured alcohol (not rubbing or grain alcohol). Keep the sealer at the same consistency as when you first open it—kind of thin, like a very light dry sherry. Remember, every time you open it and use it, some alcohol evaporates, so when it thickens the least bit, thin it with a bit of alcohol, but don't swamp it.

If protective sealer dries, yet remains slightly or just barely "tacky," don't fret; that is its bond to ally with the glue or varnish. But if it is really very sticky, it means one of three things: it is a very damp, humid, or rainy day, in which case you wait until dry weather comes; it needs thinning with denatured alcohol; or you have had it too long and it is old and tired. Protective sealer will keep for one year after you receive it freshly bottled; after that it may look and act the same, but it will not dry.

CLEANING THE SEALER BRUSH

After using your brush with protective sealer, clean it with denatured alcohol or a good brush cleaner, wash it in soap and water, reshape it, and let it dry.

7 CUTTING PRINTS

IMPORTANCE OF CUTTING: YOUR SCISSORS

Cutting is actually the most important part of decoupage. You need a pair of good scissors with thin, fine blades. I use small, fine-curved German-made surgical scissors which resemble cuticle scissors, and also import them for most of my pupils. I have used the same pair for twenty-five years, and heaven help the person who touches them! Never use your decoupage scissors for cutting anything else, and never let anyone else use them; good scissors, like gloves, mold to your hand and your way of holding them.

Scissors for decoupage can be bought at drug and department stores, or at surgical supply houses. (Also see Sources of Supply.)

36. *How I hold my trusty old scissors. I hope that you will do the same. The dingle-dangle is not affectation, but rather identification. So* NOBODY *touches!*

37. *Example of cutting. How to let the print and your hands "relax" on the table, enabling you to cut comfortably. The cutting will end on the outside edge where it started—with no uncut parts in between.*

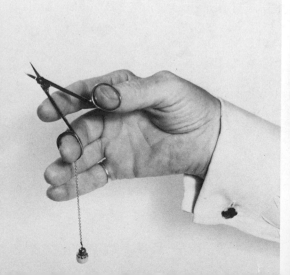

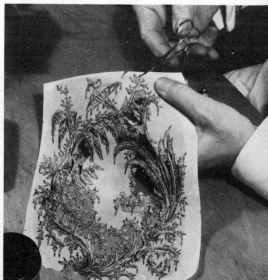

38. LEFT: *Fully-colored and partially-cut print. Notice how all the small inside "bits" are cut first.* THEN *the large inside pieces; after that, the* OUTSIDE, *starting at lower left (where the cutting will ultimately end, with everything cut!).*

39. CENTER: *The finished piece of cutting: colored, sealed, and cut all in one piece.*

40. RIGHT: *Reverse of finished cutting; proof that it should be even prettier from the back than from the front. Here there is no color or design to distract the viewer from the most important part of decoupage—cutting. "I have thirty-six of these to do for a pair of bombé commodes!" "So . . . you think you have problems?" Cut by Hiram Manning.*

HOW TO HOLD SCISSORS

Hold your scissors with your thumb and middle finger, bracing them with your index finger. The curved blades should point outward, to your right; they would only be in your way if pointed to your left. It's like walking pigeon-toed. Don't get a death grip on them either. Get yourself comfortable. Rest your elbow on the chair arm or on a table. After all, it is a piece of paper you are going to cut up—not rich Aunt Tillie's will!

HOW TO HOLD PAPER

Hold your paper in your left hand between index and middle finger, and lightly brace it with your thumb and ring finger, thumb on top. Hold it light and loose; let it almost float in your hand.

Don't make the mistake of grabbing it tensely—you'll wind up with a tired wrist and an aching arm.

AND NOW TO CUT

Cut at an even rhythm, like breathing, opening and closing your scissors at a steady rate. Don't move your scissors or your right hand, except to open and close the blades. Move the paper, turning it back and forth as you cut into the print. Feed the paper into the scissors; don't *push* the scissors into the paper.

Cut with your scissors from the middle of the blade almost to the top, but not quite. Don't go all the way to the haft of the blade and take one big slice. That is like trying to cut a soufflé with a spade!

It will take some experimenting to become accustomed to this way of cutting (like learning to pat your head and rub your tummy simultaneously). For practice, take a piece of paper in your left hand, hold it loosely, flip it and turn it from left to right and back again. Move it with your fingers, not with your wrist or arm. Move your fingers into many combinations of positions to make the paper turn easily, at your will. Continue until you have the feel of the paper—then feed it into your scissors.

Remember to cut from underneath the paper, not from the top. This keeps your hand and scissors out of the way and allows you to see what you are actually cutting, instead of trying to peer around or under a thumb. The *only* time it is permissible to cut from the top side is when the print or paper is so in your way that an attempt to cut from underneath will literally rip the print.

How to cut the small, inside sections

On many prints you will find some little inside sections that have to be cut, with no access to them from the outside. (See Figure 7.)

When you have this to contend with, punch a hole with one point of your scissors, from the top, into the paper to be cut out. Make a

outside edge
of paper
Fig. 7

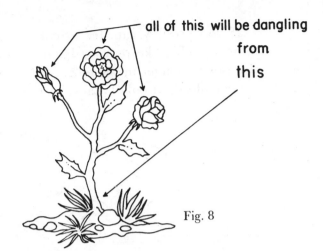

all of this will be dangling
from
this

Fig. 8

small slit, and then cut from underneath. Cut all the inside bits first, before you even begin to tackle the outside edges. The outside uncut edges of the paper give you something to hold on to.

Before you start to cut the outside edges of the print, make "bridges" with a pencil line, to hold together dangling stems, etc., to keep them from breaking off (Figure 8).

The places marked X in Figure 9 are treated as inside bits. Cut them first; then cut the outside, again leaving bridges to hold the parts together. Cut the bridges off only when you are ready to apply and glue your decoupage.

.... bridges

Fig. 9

If you possibly can, try to cut every day, even if only for five minutes. This "keeps your hand in." Don't cut when you're too tired or no longer in the mood. As with any creative undertaking, you should do it only because you want to and *must!*

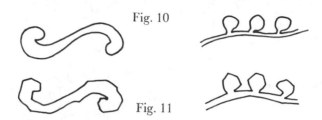

Fig. 10

Fig. 11

How to cut scrolls, berries and other round details

If you are cutting berries on a branch, or part of a scroll, as in Figure 10, try to cut it, as far as possible, in one movement. Turn your paper and cut steadily in one even motion. This will avoid a chopped or hacked-out look, as in the bad example shown in Figure 11.

How to cut leaves, grass and other pointed details

If you are cutting out a flower or tree with pointed petals, leaves, grass, or reeds (Figure 12), cut this way: cut-stop-turn; cut-stop-turn; cut-stop-turn, as in Figure 13.

If you are cutting leaves you must learn to shape them. If a leaf is like the one in Figure 14, cut it as shown on the dotted line. Your leaf will come out as shown in Figure 15. This gives it a bit more style and pizzaz!

Remember, the part you are cutting out and keeping is to your left, in your left hand, the one holding the paper. (Lefties, remember to reverse!) The part you are cutting off and discarding is to your right, in your scissors hand. Remove the cut-off parts. Long curls of useless paper are only in your way, so cut them off.

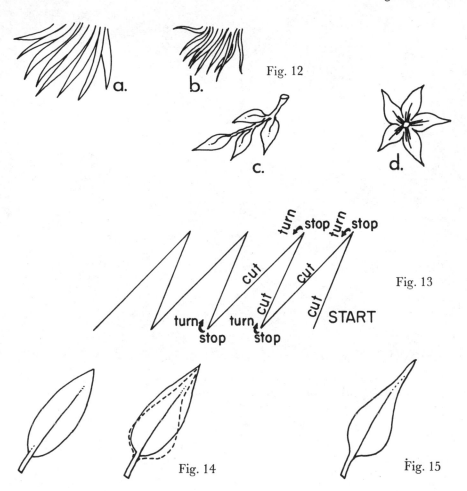

Fig. 12

Fig. 13

Fig. 14

Fig. 15

When you cut around a print, or part of it, leave every part of it behind you; cut, and end up at the point where you started, with the whole bit then cut and removed. If you come to a difficult part, don't skip it and leave it for later, because when you *do* come back to it, it's going to be twice as hard to cut. You'll have nothing to hold on to, and you may ruin it.

Right from the beginning, cut as carefully and beautifully as you can. You will eventually pick up speed, so don't worry about that now. Develop good habits in cutting.

41. *A silver chest with ground of Pompadour blue, decoupaged with original Pillement chinoiserie patterns still in print when box was designed by Maybelle Manning and executed by Mrs. Clara Friedman.*

A SUMMING-UP

Most beginners feel that cutting is rather nerve-racking, but remember it's new to you, you're tense, you haven't quite got the hang of it. Experienced cutters find it very relaxing. I know I do. It's rather like knitting. At first you are all snarled up with slipped stitches and tangled wool. Which needle goes where? Then one day you are knitting, all relaxed and watching TV, and you wonder why you made such a production of it in the first place.

Many of my pupils cut and watch TV. When I'm nervous or edgy, I cut for relaxation. Since I travel a good deal, I cut while flying. It passes the time and I get a good bit of cutting done. Someone always asks the hostess, "What's with that nut back there cutting paper dolls?" So she passes up and down the aisle, trying not to look nosey, but finally has to ask me what I'm doing. "Cutting," I say. This brings a raised eyebrow and more questions. So I explain, and it usually ends up "Instant Fascination," and I wind up with my drink served first and another prospective *découpeuse*. And both experiences are rewarding!

So do learn to cut as beautifully as you can. Truly, it is fun once you get past the first agonizing stages. The actual cutting is an exercise in visual and manual dexterity, and I hope that I have been able to give you the sense and feel of it.

Never forget that your finished decoupage is no better than your cutting, no matter how fine your finish or design.

CUTTING FOR LEFTIES

Lefties do not normally use their right hand as well as righties use their left hand—but left-handed people must learn to hold the prints and move them with their right hand, so as to cut them with the left.

Right-handed beginners tend to move their scissors instead of the paper, and possibly it is even more difficult for a leftie to turn the paper in his right hand—but both must learn the reverse process. It is necessary for the detailed cutting of fine prints.

I never believe in "forcing" a left-handed person to cut a certain way, but I have found that most left-handed persons cut best with the method I shall describe—and the exceptions, alas, will just have to work it out for themselves. I have taught more than a thousand lefties to cut this way and many of them are among my very best cutters. Begin as follows:

1. Hold scissors in left hand, points or curve of scissors pointing out to your left. Normally you will cut from the *left* edge of the paper.
2. Hold the paper in your right hand. Turn the paper, do not move the scissors in your left hand except to open and close them; this is difficult, but just as difficult for a right-handed person, with the paper in his left hand.
3. The part you are cutting out and keeping is in your *right* hand and the part you are discarding, or cutting off, slides into your left, or scissors, hand as you cut.
4. In brief, if you were cutting a flower, you would hold it in your *right* hand, turning it with that hand and cutting from the *left* side of the flower, with your paper discard moving to your left, or into your scissors hand.
5. One more word for you lefties: When paper is turned sharply to the *right,* and a difficult situation arises in which you can't cut from underneath without tearing the paper (or print), then you must come "over" the paper, and, as soon as possible, come back down "under" and cut from underneath. Happy cutting!

WHEN TO USE KNIFE-CUTTING

Many people, including teachers of decoupage, think that decoupage is a form of knife cutting. It is not. Knife-cutting has its place, yes, but not as the mainstay of fine cutting. It is an adjunct only. A dramatic effect that you can achieve with the use of a knife is the cutting out, from a print, of a series of windowpanes in a building; you can then back them with foil which, showing through the windowpanes, gives the look of an illumination. Using the knife in making a tiny slit for illumination is also fine. But for curves, forming a rose or figure, a leaf or petal—though it can be done with a knife—it is the hard and slow way. Knife cuttings end up angular and stiff, so when you want this effect in certain prints, use the knife by all means.

I have had pupils in classes who were devotees of knife-cutting. They refused instruction on how to use scissors, and stubbornly stuck to the knife even though I was there to teach them the scissors way. Result? All the other pupils had their prints colored, cut and glued in while the knife devotees were still cutting, slit by slit.

I use knife cutting on thick paper or pasteboard as a form of sculpting. My purpose is to raise the top of the paper from its background, thereby adding a three-dimensional quality. The result is best used under glass, or framed as a thing in itself.

You must have a sharp knife, and use it only where the paper is thick enough to be lifted in layers. My way is similar to pin-pricking, but instead of using a needle, you raise a piece of paper with a knife.

You can give a velvety look to paper by cutting light slits very close together with a knife, literally giving it a nap. The closer you make the cuts, and the less diagonal they are, the more nap you will raise (Figure 16). The paper has to be of a very fine grain and heavy enough for you to be able to cut and lift without cutting through it. (Figure 17.) Cut on the diagonal, as shown in Figure 18.

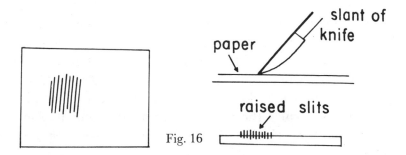

Fig. 16

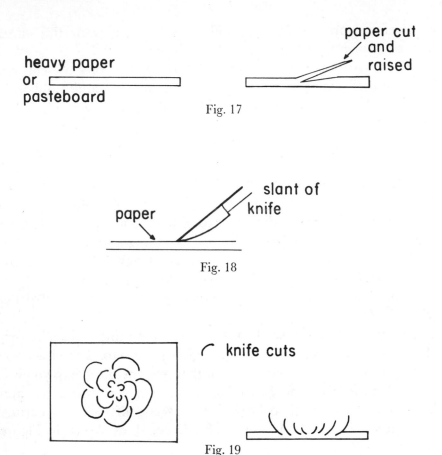

Fig. 17

Fig. 18

Fig. 19

Say you are raising the petal of a flower (Figure 19). The paper is still held intact, but the petals are cut and raised from it without your cutting through to the back of the paper. Notice that each petal is cut separately and that no two slits join. This is important.

Most ready-colored prints are not on the proper pasteboard for knife cutting. You can do knife-cutting freehand on blank paper or you can hand color the paper first, and then cut it; sometimes you can glue the print to the proper cardboard first and then knife cut it.

 GLUING

There are hundreds of glues on the market, each good for certain things—plastic glues for plastics, stamp glue for stamps, furniture glue for furniture, right down to good old flour-and-water paste for kids to make on rainy days. But for fine decoupage you need something else. The glue must be transparent, nonstaining, easy to clean off, and it must stick when *you* want it to and are ready, not before; in other words, it must be flexible. A glue that sticks at once is hopeless for fine, elaborate decoupage. That doesn't mean the glue is wrong, but that it is wrongly used.

Let's take an example. Say you are decoupaging a coffee table and want a border of scrolls or leaves, and you want to start with a bowknot at the center bottom edge. You've colored and cut the bowknot beautifully. You stick it on, and it's *stuck,* but it's crooked or off-center. And you are stuck *with* it, too! You've got to move it, but can't without ruining it. So you have to tear it off and wreck it. There goes an hour of love, cutting, coloring, and your disposition.

Suppose you had a glue with which you could glue that bowknot on and move it, pick it up, put it down again, twist it, turn it, until it is exactly where you think you want it, and then—an hour, a day, or a month later—change your mind and decide you want it a bit higher or lower, to the left or right, or, *'raus mit;* suppose you could simply wet it, remove it without harming either the bowknot or the background, and reglue it as good as new. Wouldn't all you *découpeurs* and *découpeuses* be happy? Well, I have such a glue. It is my plain old "all-purpose glue," (see Sources of Supply).

MATERIALS

All-purpose glue (see Sources of Supply)
Small curved scissors

Tweezers
One square inch of ordinary kitchen sponge (not the fine or rubber kind)
One small bowl of water
Paper towels (for hands)

METHOD

These particular instructions are for gluing decoupage on any prepared surface, including glass. (For *under* glass, see "Decoupage Under Glass.")

1. *Always put your glue on the object to be glued, not on the paper.* That is rule number 1!
2. Spread the glue with your finger and work it into the surface. Don't use globs of it. Just spread and work a film of glue over the prepared surface, then dip your finger in water and work that in. Keep adding water and working it in until the surface feels like oil or melted butter. Work it as if you were greasing a pan. If the glue separates and leaves dry spots or circles of "no glue," you have used too much water. Add a

42. *If your print is partially glued to the box and it won't fit, cut and make it fit! At the author's left, note print with "bridges" as described in text discussion of inside sections. These are snipped off at this time—just before gluing.*

43. *How to "roll" and "press" (Method, 6) without pushing.*

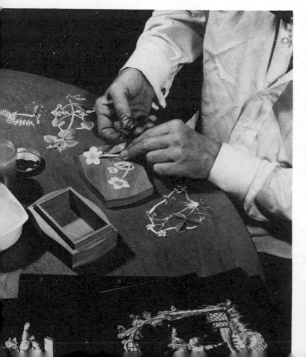

bit more glue until it holds together again. You want a surface of glue on which you can literally slide your cutouts around.

3. When it is at that stage, rinse your fingers in water to remove the glue, and dry them. Now pick up your cutting or cuttings and place them on the glued surface. Don't mash them down instantly. Move each cutout into the exact position you want. Keep it loose and move or twist it with your fingers, tweezers, the points of your small scissors, or anything, to get that particular piece of cutting *exactly* where you want it. Then add the next piece, move, turn, and lift that piece until it is where you want it.

4. If you decide you don't want the piece you have applied, as it is not quite right for that spot, take it off, rinse it in water to remove glue, pat it dry with tissue, and put it aside until you do want it.

5. If your glued surface starts to dry or gets too sticky, moisten it with a damp sponge. Sometimes you might have to add a bit more glue to the spot you have just removed that cutting from. Get it like oil again, and continue.

6. Now, if all your design "of the moment" is placed exactly where you think you want it, take your small piece of sponge, dip it in water and wring it out well. Lightly tamp your design down with it. Rinse the sponge and wring it out again. This time use it to keep your fingers moist. Moisten your fingers on the sponge, and roll and press your design down with your finger. Be firm about it, but don't push or you'll move your design out of place. Press and roll from the center of the cutting out to the edges. Press and roll delicate stems, small leaves, etc., the way *they* go; follow their contour.

Don't forget to keep your fingers moist, or the decoupage will stick to you instead of to the object. Rinse the sponge out from time to time as it becomes sticky, and always wring it almost dry. Rinse your fingers, dry them, and then moisten them on the sponge again. The idea is to keep your fingers and hands clean and damp, *not wet.*

7. When everything is glued down, use your fingernail (whichever one is easiest for you) and, keeping it damp with the sponge, press along the edges of the cutting with the flat of your nail, to get the edges down as tightly as possible. When you think everything is down tight, hold the object at eye level against the light and turn it in all directions. You'll find lots of little loose edges thumbing their noses at you. So, thumb back, and flatten 'em with your fingernail and/or with more glue if necessary. *Do not use a roller!* It is too hard and presses out practically all the glue. Use your fingers, and no matter how hard you press they will leave enough glue to hold the design. Your fingers are softer and more sensitive than any tool.

8. When the design is practically bonded to the surface, glued *down,* not merely on, and no loose edges are flapping anywhere, wipe off the excess glue from the *undecorated* parts (*not* from what you have just glued on) with your clean, damp piece of sponge. Always keep the sponge wrung out and clean; a dirty, gluey sponge will smear the glue around without removing it.

9. Let the freshly glued design set at least an hour to compose itself and dry. If you clean it off right away, while the glue is still fresh and unset, you will remove too much of it and it will "leach" out from under the paper. It will appear stuck, from water suction, but the prints come loose under varnish a month or so later. They rise up like bubbles under the varnish. (Don't panic: the cure for that comes under "Pitfalls, Disasters, and Their Cure"; but the best thing is not to make the mistake in the first place.)

You see, your paper itself is still damp from the glue and the sponge, and the water from the sponge will go right down through it, like through net, and wash out the glue underneath. Besides, with the paper still damp, the sponge, in cleaning off the glue, will cause all those little edges to act up again. So let it be for an hour or two, or until the next day if you don't feel like doing it then. Sometimes I clean it the same day, and sometimes I'm not in the mood, so I do it mañana.

10. When the glued design has had a siesta and is well-set and dry, get a bowl of clean, hot water, as hot as is comfortable, but don't scald yourself. Take the same old piece of sponge, dip it in the hot water, and wring it out again, so it is as dry as possible. Drops of water will be on your fingertips, so touch your fingers to a paper towel to remove the water or it will flood a small leaf or scroll and cause it to unglue.

Now start to remove the glue from the top of your applied design and its edges. Don't wipe it as if it were a plate, or scrub it like a pan. Tender loving care is the idea. Press the hot sponge to the design and sort of twist the sponge and lift it once or twice. Turn it over to the clean side and repeat. Then rinse it and wring it out again. Get the drops of water off your fingers on the towel, and repeat. Do a small area at a time until it is almost squeaky clean, but *never let it get wet!* I use the sponge in one hand and a dry tissue in the other. In other words, I sponge and blot. You can wipe gently and carefully *away* from the edges, but never toward them or you will rough them up and lift them.

CHANGING YOUR MIND

Do *not* put protective sealer on until you are completely satisfied with your design and it is thoroughly dry. If there is one small piece of cutting that bothers you, take your sponge, *wet* this time, and squeeze enough water to wet and flood that particular spot. Let it soak a bit one minute, two minutes, maybe three, then gently poke at an edge of it with the point of your scissors or tweezers. Don't force it! When it is ready, you can lift it right off without harming the piece of cutting or your ground. Blot the ground dry with tissue. Rinse the cutting in water to remove glue. Blot it dry and put it aside for future use. Pick out a cutting you *do* want in the spot.

The edges of the other cuttings adjoining that spot will be wet and loose. Dry and lift these edges and reglue them. Again put glue on that empty spot and place your new piece there, following the same procedure for gluing it that you originally used. Let dry, clean off, and there you are, ready to go again, and nothing ruined or wasted.

Removing sealer

If you have put on protective sealer and are dissatisfied, brush that spot with denatured alcohol to remove the sealer. Blot with tissue, and then proceed as above.

9 DECOUPAGE UNDER VARNISH

MATERIALS

Maché varnish. (See Sources of Supply.)

One-half-inch, *soft* (squirrel, sable, badger), flat brush for most pieces; a two-inch brush for large screens or dining room tables.

A couple of flat-topped jars (or cans) to set small varnished pieces on to dry.

Newspaper (to keep drips and splatters off the table or floor).

X-acto knife.

VARNISHING IN BRIEF

Apply varnish only after your decoupage piece is glued down, cleaned off, and has had a coat of protective sealer (but do not seal oil gold leaf surfaces.) Never varnish on a damp or rainy day, unless you are working in an air-conditioned room.

1. Dip your brush in the varnish and flow the varnish onto the object, not back and forth, but in one direction only, using short, quick strokes. Feather each stroke back into the area wet with varnish, so the strokes all blend together.

2. Varnish the most accessible exterior surfaces first. Wipe up any drips that may gather at the edges, using your finger or brush.

3. From time to time, when the brush becomes too full of varnish, wipe it on the lip of the varnish jar.

4. Let the varnished pieces dry in the open for at least 24 hours before applying the next coat. Then press hard with your finger; if no marks remain, add another coat of varnish.
5. Apply a minimum of 20 coats of varnish. Let each one dry for 24 hours. Press with your fingers to test for dryness.
6. If you are using maché varnish, do not sand between coats, as the varnish makes its own bond and all the coats become as one. With other varnishes follow manufacturer's directions.

Care of varnish

If you do not keep enough pieces of decoupage going and ready for varnishing to use up the whole jar of maché varnish at one time, here is my tip to keep it from going sour: once the jar is opened and partially used, the varnish will tend to thicken from the air in the jar, no matter how tight the lid is on. Pour the remainder into a smaller jar until the jar is brimful of varnish and cap it. This way it will keep perfectly. If your varnish should thicken before you do this, you can thin it with a bit of pure gum turpentine. If the varnish has set like jello, it is too far gone.

VARNISHING A BOX

1. First do the rims or top edges of the box, the part where the hinges go or where the top (lid) and bottom edges come together when the box is hinged.
2. When the edges are done, turn the box over, and, holding it in your left hand *inside* the box, (the box is now upside-

44. *Back view of antique English walnut knife box, circa 1790. Mrs. W. James Moore.*

down on the left hand) varnish its top (the lid) or the bottom of the box proper. Flow the varnish on and lay it with short strokes, lightly, again, not brushing it back and forth but laying it on in one direction only, *feathering* the brush back into the part previously applied. Go all over the surface this way until it is almost, but not quite, a "lake" of varnish.

3. Now tackle the sides. Lay your varnish on as horizontally as possible. Wipe your brush off on both sides, on the edge of the varnish jar, to remove excess varnish. Quickly and lightly stroke the brush from the top edge to the bottom edge of the box, lightly pulling the varnish down. Wipe the brush on the lip of the varnish jar from time to time when the brush becomes too full of varnish. Continue this way until that side is done, then gently pull the varnish from the bottom up, the same way. Wipe off any drips that may be on the bottom edge and proceed in this manner all the way around the box, side by side.

4. When the entire box has been varnished, place it upside down on a jar, with the inside of the box or lid resting on the jar. Since only the outside has been varnished, the inside is dry and can rest on the jar. Never place it flat on a table or surface as the outside surfaces will stick and mess up your work, and the table as well! Keep all the varnished surfaces free, as in Figure 20. If any drips appear on the bottom edge of the box, wipe them off with your finger or brush.

5. Let the varnished pieces dry this way for at least 24 hours before applying the next coat, and even then test it with your finger, pressing hard, to be sure it is dry. If no finger marks remain, continue varnishing. *Twenty coats of varnish is the absolute minimum.* Otherwise you cannot rub down without hitting or sanding off part of your paper.

6. When edges and paper are sunk under varnish, rubbing down will come out smooth, yet with paper still under varnish.

There is no need to sand between coats with maché varnish;

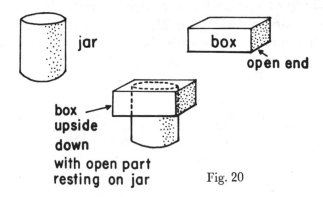

jar

box

open end

box
upside
down
with open part
resting on jar   Fig. 20

it makes it own bond and all the coats become one. With other varnishes it is best to follow the manufacturer's directions. Don't worry about lumps and bumps. The more coats of varnish you put on, the worse it will look, but it is only temporary. If dust should fall on it, wipe it off before giving it another coat of varnish. Remember to put your decoupage where it will get sufficient air to dry.

If you get drips after the varnish has dried, slice them off at varnish level with a razor or an X-acto knife. Be careful not to go *below* varnish level. The underneath surfaces will be wet and sticky. Let them dry and continue varnishing.

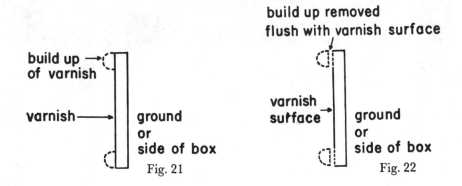

build up →
of varnish

varnish——→

ground
or
side of box
Fig. 21

build up removed
flush with varnish surface

varnish
surface →

ground
or
side of box
Fig. 22

If a buildup of varnish forms at one or both edges of the piece after many coats, as in Figure 21, take a razor or X-acto knife and pare the buildups flush with the varnished surface, as in Figure 22. Let dry and go on varnishing.

45. Louis XV poudreuse or lady's dressing-table. Pillement figures and flowers in peacock palette, on ground of Venetian yellow and Pompadour blue. Designed by the Mannings. Mrs. Stephen L. French, South Swansea, Mass.

If maché varnish should craze, don't worry. Let it dry until the wrinkles are dry too. Don't panic and sand it before it dries in an effort to get it smooth again—it will leave dark sanding-marks in the soft varnish. Test for dryness with your finger and go on varnishing. The wrinkles will eventually disappear as you add more coats of varnish.

Only when the decoupage piece is more than well-sunk under the varnish, after at least twenty coats, and is completely dry, are you ready to sand it.

VARNISHING FURNITURE

1. Remove any hardware and drawers first. Treat drawers as a flat surface or top.
2. Put a lightly hammered-in large tack on the bottom of each leg of the piece to prevent its touching the paper you have under it to catch splatters or drips of varnish. This will prevent a sticky buildup of varnish there, so the legs or feet won't

46. *Round dining-room table, extended with two leaves. Note that the decoupage forms a complete design; the same is true with only one leaf added, and also when the table is round, or closed. Thanks to the hospitality of Nobel Prize winner Dr. William P. Murphy and his wife, this table hasn't "cooled off" in fifteen years, and it's still as good as new. Designed by Maybelle Manning. Mrs. William P. Murphy, Brookline, Mass.*

47. *Back view of a small bombé three-drawer commode.*

stick to the paper. (See Figure 23.) You must drive the tack in far enough so it will not wobble and collapse, but not so far that it will be impossible to get out again. There must be air space between the bottom of the leg and the surface.

3. Varnish the top as you would the top of a box.
4. Varnish the sides horizontally, then lightly pull down, then up, exactly as you would the sides of a box.
5. If you have carvings to contend with, pull the varnish away from their edges as you would the inside bottom edge of a box or tray.
6. Do not varnish sides of drawers or they will stick.

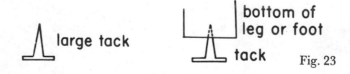

large tack

bottom of
leg or foot

tack

Fig. 23

VARNISHING A TRAY OR THE INSIDE OF A BOX

1. Varnish the lip or gallery of the tray or side of box first. Varnish it horizontally, following the contour of the tray or side of box.
2. Before you tackle the ground, or bottom, of the tray or box, pull your varnish away from where the gallery or lip joins the bottom of the tray, or where side of box joins bottom. Pull it out onto the bottom with your varnish brush, as much as you can, almost scrubbing it out with your brush. This is to avoid a buildup of varnish there, which is difficult to sand out.
3. Apply your varnish as you would on the outside top or bottom of a box, making your "lake" of varnish on the bottom of the tray or box.

VARNISHING A SHADOW·BOX OR PICTURE

For varnishing anything where the varnish and the glass abut, and the glass cannot be removed, extend the varnish about an inch out onto the glass as you varnish. (There is method in this madness.) In sanding the varnish down, the glass will get scratched badly unless there is something to shield it, and the varnish will protect the glass from the sandpaper, and after it is all sanded and ready for waxing:

Take your sharpest X-acto knife and cut straight down through the varnish, where the edge of the decoupage under varnish joins the glass. Then scrape up to that cut, with your X-acto knife, to remove the excess varnish on the glass, exactly as you would remove excess paint from a window sash.

If you have steady hands, this will leave you with a neat, varnished edge, abutting your glass. Get the glass scraped thoroughly clean. Wax your decoupage edge and there you are.

48. *One of a set of four antique Venetian chairs owned by the author. Decoupage of hand-colored French flowers, ribbons, and tambourines in blues, yellows and greens on ground of pale celadon green. Carved borders in Venetian yellow, with shells and cartouches in Pompadour blue; tambourines inset with mother-of-pearl. The Mannings. In author's collection.*

VARNISH PROBLEMS AND THEIR SOLUTIONS

1. For drips that show after the varnish has dried: Slice them off *at varnish level,* (not below) with a razor blade or an X-acto knife. They will be mushy and sticky inside, as will the surface under them. Let the surfaces dry, then continue varnishing.

2. For build-up of varnish: With a razor or an X-acto knife, pare the buildups flush with the varnished surface, as in Figure 22. Let dry and continue varnishing.

3. For varnish crazes: It sometimes happens that the varnish crazes and looks like a wrinkled old apple. Don't lose your cool. Don't sand it. Just let everything, including the wrinkles dry so thoroughly that no marks show when pressed firmly with your finger. When dry, continue varnishing. The wrinkles will eventually disappear under the coats of varnish.

4. Varnish vs. lacquer: All varnishes are lacquers, but not all lacquers are varnishes. The bases of all of them are "lacs," certain gums or oils. Varnish is slower-drying, more elastic, and it tones a color. Lacquer is quicker-drying, much brittler and clearer. Dampness slows the drying of and drying out of varnish. Dampness, on the other hand, *speeds* the drying of lacquer and dries it out, too.

Lacquer and glue are basically at daggers drawn, in spite of Coromandel screens. That's why the screens fall apart or are so devilish to keep in good condition. Glue wants to go down and lacquer wants to pull up, and something eventually gives way. That is why I use varnish; it is more amenable to decoupage.

But there is varnish, and there is varnish for decoupage. There is outdoor varnish, indoor varnish, furniture varnish, floor varnish,

49. *Baby grand piano. Inside of lid decoupaged with Venetian scene after Turner; Boucher cupids playing various musical instruments around edge. Decoupage in Sanguine tones with yellow, on ground of Pompadour blue. Designed by Hiram Manning; executed by Mrs. A. Ware Bosworth, Cambridge, Mass. (Photograph courtesy of Addison Gallery of American Art, Phillips Andover Academy, Andover, Mass.)*

bar varnish, deck varnish for yachts, and so on. Good as they may be for their purpose, none of them is designed for twenty, thirty or more successive coats. They build up a tension after too many coats and finally pull away from their base. Ask anyone who has ever varnished a boatdeck too often, without removing the old

50. *Sliding drop-front "piano" desk in Pompadour blue, with dancing figures from a "Fête champêtre." Writing surface of paper marquetry in gold and tortoiseshell paper. Mrs. Kimball Powning.*

varnish, or a house painter who has put just one too many coats of paint on a house without burning off the old paint. It lifts, it cracks, it chips and pulls away; in any case, something goes wrong with it

51. Antique Venetian bombé commode. Baroque cartouches in bronze tones. Boucher cupids hand colored in Sanguine, with Pillement chinoiserie flowers in peacock tones. Ground of Venetian yellow, bordered with Venetian green. Executed by the Mannings for the late Mrs. George Skakel; now in the possession of her daughter, Mrs. George Terrien.

52. *White alabaster jar with ormolu (metal) mountings. Note how the alabaster quality is maintained even under twenty coats of varnish. Decoupage of Pillement flowers and foliage in 18th Century Palette; baroque figures in Grisaille. Mrs. W. James Moore.*

because it just was not designed for that many coats, and although some varnishes stay down for a long while, eventually they will give way.

Sometimes a varnish, clear as crystal to begin with, will turn foggy after more coats than it was designed for. Some varnishes will look flat and dull; others take on a varnishy look, as if they need air. If your ability to see the decoupage as a whole is affected in any way by the appearance of the varnish, it is not right. It is like champagne in a plastic glass. It is still champagne, it's good and you'll drink it, but it would be infinitely better in a crystal glass, where you could see the bubbles sparkle and dance.

WHAT A GOOD VARNISH SHOULD DO

A proper varnish for decoupage, properly applied, rubbed down, waxed and polished, should give the decoupage an inner glow, as if a light were coming from within it. You should not be conscious of the varnish at all. Though a well-varnished piece of decoupage makes you feel that you can reach down and touch the design, what you actually do touch is a silken smooth surface that has no quality of varnish about it.

When my students and I show our work in art shows and decoupage exhibitions, the inevitable question we hear is, "What makes your work glow like that? It's as though the glow came from inside it!" The answer is the maché varnish, (see Sources of Supply), and, to a degree, the coloring.

The late Francis Taylor of the Metropolitan Museum called my finish one of the most exciting things he had seen in this century. He said, "I see it. I touch it. But I don't believe it. It's all but immoral."

SANDING OR RUBBING DOWN

MATERIALS

Wet or dry Tri-m-ite sandpaper (black) in three grades or grits:
No. 280-A, the coarsest, for first sanding
No. 400, for second sanding
No. 600, for polishing
Steel wool #0000 for buffing
Bowl of water for wetting sandpaper
Paper towels, napkins, or tissues, to wipe up with as you sand your decoupage

METHOD

Before you start to sand, be sure your decoupage is well sunk under the varnish, with an absolute minimum of twenty coats. If you do any less, you will hit paper while sanding!

Cut sandpaper sheets into eight equal pieces and fold each piece in half, grit side out. Each piece of sandpaper has its number or grit printed on the back. When you cut up your sandpaper, see that the number is on the back of each piece. If it is not, mark the number with pencil on the back. This will avoid confusion as to which grit it is.

Start with No. 280-A, the coarsest. Wet the sandpaper in the water and start sanding your decoupage, keeping the piece itself and the sandpaper wet—not damp, but sopping *wet*. With the wet sandpaper in your hand, sand one surface at a time in a small circular motion, first doing one small area, then overlapping onto the next.

Use a good, firm pressure. Scrub or scour, as you would a burnt pot or pan. Don't worry about ruining your work. If you have enough varnish on it, nothing is going to happen except that the surface will get sanded flat and even, which is what you want. If, by any horrible chance, you do hit paper, *stop* at once and look up "Pitfalls, Disasters and Their Cures" (see Index), for a solution.

From time to time the water on the piece will get very milky from the sanded-off varnish. Wipe it off with Kleenex or similar tissues, wet the paper and surface again, and go on sanding. Sand until the surface is flat, with no little dents or depressions in it.

When it is flat, wipe the piece dry with tissue and hold or tip it against the light. You will probably see little bright, shiny spots. Sand again until they are completely gone. The piece may feel completely smooth to you in spite of the shiny spots; nevertheless sand them out, for when you finally wax your piece, they will loom large, and you will wish you had removed them. Don't worry if the work takes on a moiré look. It is usual at this stage.

When sanding, do the edges of the piece last. Most people tend to let the sandpaper run over and around the edge in a rounded kind of way, but, if you leave the edges for last, you won't go through paint as well as varnish, and ruin your work.

When your folded sandpaper has been used up on one side, turn it over. When the second side is no longer working, take a fresh piece. Sandpaper is cheaper than wasted elbow grease.

Don't sand until your fingers are all raw and sore. If you can work comfortably in gloves, wear heavy-duty rubber gloves, the cloth-lined type. (I find that gloves get in my way, but I can't garden with them either; however, you may find them helpful in saving your manicure and your hands.)

When your piece of decoupage looks and feels flat and smooth, with not even one tiny bright shiny spot showing, use No. 400 sandpaper to remove and polish out any slight scratches that might be there. Use it the same way as the No. 280-A, very wet. When the water becomes milky, wipe it off and wet it again with clean water. Apply a lighter pressure than you used with the coarser sandpaper. This step is to smooth the surface, not to sand it flat as at first.

When the surfaces become twice as smooth as before, take the No. 600 sandpaper, *wet,* and polish the surface about a minute or two, until it feels like satin. Wipe it off and rinse clean with a fresh damp tissue or sponge; dry. Now polish with steel wool #0000. Use the steel wool *dry* with very *light* pressure. Don't be heavy-handed at this stage or you will scratch the polished surface.

When it is thoroughly polished, smooth as cream, wipe off the grit or steel wool particles with dry tissue, then a damp sponge, and polish it dry with the palm of your hand. It should feel even smoother than ivory. Be sure that *all* the steel-wool particles are removed or they will make gritty bits in your matte final finish, which you are now ready to apply.

APPLYING MATTE FINISH

MATERIALS

One bottle matte final finish
One half-inch soft, flat brush

METHOD

After your decoupage is rubbed down per instructions, apply three thin coats of matte final finish, one coat a day. Remember, don't varnish on damp or rainy days unless your room is air-conditioned.

At the bottom of the jar of matte final finish there will be a thin film of gummy goo. Be sure that the goo is thoroughly stirred up and incorporated back into the liquid. It is an essential part of it. Don't shake the bottle—stir it, or you'll get air bubbles; they're nice in pop and champagne, but for varnish, no! Then, with your half-inch brush, apply the matte to the edges or rims of your box.

Flip the box over and put your left hand inside it to hold it. Varnish the bottom or top (lid) of the box in light, quick strokes, feathering your brush back into the wet area. Don't brush back and forth; brush in one direction only. When the surface is covered, as quickly as possible brush lightly from end to end so that there are no brush marks or strokes or ridges of varnish. Float your brush as you might imagine Pavlova floated across a stage!

Then do the sides, horizontally first. Then lightly, like swans-down, pull the varnish down and do *not* brush it back up. You want to work the matte as little as possible and achieve the smoothest coat possible. When you are through with the matte, let the box dry, perched on something like a jar as in the regular varnish instructions. (See Figure 20 under "Decoupage Under Varnish.")

If you are applying matte to the inside of a box or piece, do it in the same way as you would varnish the inside of a box, only lighter and quicker.

Do the edges first, then the sides horizontally, lightly pulling the matte down to the inside bottom; pull and brush the matte away from edges and corners where they join the bottom, and out onto the bottom. Then lightly and quickly varnish the bottom and brush from the end lightly, to eliminate brush strokes and any varnish ridges.

Give it three coats of matte allowing twenty-four hours between each coat. When the last coat is dry, you are ready for its final sanding and polishing.

Sanding the Matte Finish

MATERIALS

> No. 600 Wet or dry Tri-m-ite black sandpaper, cut into eight equal pieces and folded with sand side out
> steel wool #0000
> Bowl of water
> Paper napkins or tissues

METHOD

Take your No. 600 sandpaper, dip it in water, *wet,* and lightly sand off the dust bumps or gritty bits. Don't sand any more than that.

Sand in light, small circular motions, leaving the edges till last. Just get it feeling smooth with all the gritty feeling gone! And no more, or you'll sand the matte right off, and will have wasted three days. In case you do, sand it *all* off and start the three-coat bit all over again.

When the gritty feeling is gone, wipe the surface off with dry tissue. Rinse it with a damp clean sponge. Dry it again with tissue, and your decoupage will now look slightly ill, with dull spots where grit was removed and shiny spots elsewhere.

Now get out the steel wool #0000. That's the cure. Use the dry steel wool lightly, as lightly as if it were your own face you were rubbing. Of course you have to use some pressure, but rub *lightly* in a small circular motion until the surface is uniformly dull, with no shiny bits here and there. When it is uniformly dull, *stop!*

Wipe steel wool particles off with dry tissue, then a damp sponge. Really polish it with the heel or palm of your hand, briskly, the way English butlers used to buff silver. It should then feel like almost the smoothest thing you ever touched. Now you are ready to wax it if the surface is *dead flat dry*. I usually wait a day or two before I wax mine.

Bet you thought you'd never make it this far, didn't you?

WAXING A FINISHED DECOUPAGE

MATERIALS

Wax—a good paste furniture wax.
Small soft cloth 3″ by 3″ for applying wax
Bowl of cold water
Soft piece of cloth for polishing.

Any fine paste furniture wax will do, but not liquid wax, in my opinion. Of course, some pastes are better than others. Choose the one you like best. Personally, I use Goddard's English Paste Wax.

METHOD

Here is how I wax a varnished decoupage object. Take a piece of very soft cloth about three inches by three inches, fold it into a flat pad, dip it in cold water, squeeze some water out (you want it more wet than damp), and rub it on the wax, just enough to get a very small amount of wax on it. Apply it to the surface to be waxed, rubbing in a brisk circular motion. Add more wax from time to time as needed, and keep the cloth wettish. Don't get too much wax on at a time or things will tend to get gummy.

I polish this way with the wet cloth and very little wax until the surface begins to shine even when wet. Then, with the dry polishing cloth, I buff it as briskly and quickly as possible. Quick and light is the idea. A first waxing sometimes does not take evenly all over, so repeat until it does.

Wax or buff the piece from time to time thereafter, perhaps when you polish furniture. This will build up its patina and make it even more beautiful, and protect it, too; waxed this way, finger smudges, etc., can easily be removed by wiping with a damp anything and buffing with a soft cloth.

Now, if it's a box, you can glue in your cloth lining. Put the hinges back on (if you can remember where you put them), and the box is done!

So stand back and admire it, and if you have a smug, self-satisfied expression on your face, *I'm with you!*

Summary for Decoupage Under Varnish

1. Brush one coat of protective sealer on the tray or other surface (properly prepared) that you plan to decoupage. Allow to dry (about ten to fifteen minutes, depending on weather).

2. Apply two, three or more coats of paint—as many as necessary to cover. The thinner the paint the better; four thin coats are better than one thick coat. Allow to dry overnight between coats.

3. Give painted surface a thin, well-brushed-out coat of protective sealer. Allow to dry.

4. Give *any* print you plan to cut (bought already colored, or one you have colored) a coat of protective sealer and blot dry immediately with crumpled facial tissue. Do this *before* you cut it out. Apply protective sealer to the *right* side of the print always, not the back of the print. If any print comes through from the back (prints from magazines, etc., sometimes do), it is *not* usable for decoupage.

For ornamental papers (book end paper, marbleized, etc.), apply one thin coat of protective sealer on front side and blot dry.

Give gold braid and gold and silver tea paper a coat of maché varnish on *back* of paper and wipe dry with tissue.

Give front side a thin, stingy, well-brushed-out coat of maché varnish and do *not* wipe. Allow to dry.

5. When you are ready to apply your design, give the surface a *thin* coat of all-purpose glue, possibly with a dab or two of water, worked in with your fingers to give it the consistency of heavy oil, just as you would grease a pan.

6. Apply your design. Tap it down with a well-wrung-out piece of sponge.

Press it down skin tight with your finger, rolling from the center of your design out to the edges, to remove excess glue from *under* your design. Press edges tight with back of moistened fingernail.

7. When all is tight, let dry for two to three hours, then remove *all* excess glue from surface *and top* of prints, with sponge well-wrung-out in *hot* water; pat dry with tissue. Be sure *all* glue is removed from surfaces. Allow design to dry at least one hour. For gold braid, use appliqué glue and remove excess *at once!*

8. After design is *all* on and tight, all excess glue removed, and everything perfectly dry, apply a *thin,* well-brushed-out coat of protective sealer over everything. Allow to dry.

9. Apply varnish, using a soft, flat one-half-inch-wide brush. Flow on varnish generously; slurp it on! Then remove any drips or puddles from edges or corners, with wiped-off brush, before varnish sets. They are not *too* important, but best to avoid if possible. Apply a coat once a day, but never on rainy or damp days. Twenty full coats are an absolute minimum—more are better—before you begin to rub down.

10. When design is completely sunk under varnish and you feel no heavy ridges or hollows, you are ready to rub down. For the *first* sanding use No. 280-A Wet or dry Tri-m-ite sandpaper. Use it wet—soping wet—and rub down till surface is perfectly flat, with no bright, shiny pits showing. Don't worry about a moiré look—that's par for the course.

If you hit paper—*stop*—you do not have enough varnish. Re-varnish with as many coats as you deem necessary, and rub down again, until perfectly flat.

11. You are then ready for the second rubbing, using 400 Wet or dry Tri-m-ite sandpaper this time. Use the sandpaper wet, polish until satin smooth; clean off dirty water.

12. For the third rubbing use 600 Wet or dry Tri-m-ite sandpaper, wet, and polish till smooth as ivory; clean off thoroughly with damp sponge; dry. Polish with steel wool #0000 using it *dry,* and with *light* pressure in circular motion till smoother than smooth. Dust and wipe off *all* steel wool particles.

13. Apply three thin coats of Matte Final Finish Varnish, allowing 24 hours between coats.

14. Rub lightly, *very lightly,* with No. 600 Wet or dry Tri-m-ite sandpaper, using it wet, and rub just till dust lumps and gritty feel are gone—NO MORE!

15. Wipe and dry. It will be covered with dull spots. Polish lightly with *dry* steel wool #0000 till uniformly dull. Clean thoroughly to remove all steel wool particles.

16. Wax with any good paste wax (I use Goddard's). Apply wax with a

soft cloth wrung out in cold water. Use as little wax as possible, the less the better. Rub wax in thoroughly over entire surface, polish *lightly* and *briskly* with a soft lintless cloth, until surface is shining. Repeat if necessary until entire surface is evenly polished and glowing.

And I'm right there with you as you stand back to admire it—sore wrist, damp brow and all!

La rue

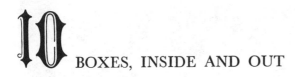 BOXES, INSIDE AND OUT

HOW TO COVER A BOX WITH PAPER

MATERIALS

Paper cut as per instructions
Protective sealer and brush
All-purpose glue
Bowl of water
1 small piece of sponge
Paper towels

METHOD

1. Seal the decorated side of the paper with protective sealer and allow to dry fifteen to twenty minutes; then it is ready for use. For most papers, apply the seal on the decorated side. However, if you are using gold or silver tea paper, seal the *back* of the paper with a generous, well-brushed-in coat of maché varnish. Then wipe it thoroughly dry with paper napkins, towels, or tissues. Turn it over to the gold or silver side and apply the stingiest, thinnest coat of maché varnish possible, as if it were the last drop in the bucket and you had to make it do. Do not wipe it off; let it dry; then it is ready for use.

2. Prepare the box. Remove the hinges and screws and put them carefully away. (They won't be needed again until the box is completely finished: varnished, rubbed down, and waxed.) Your box is now in two pieces: the box and its lid. Give the pieces (new, or stripped) an allover coat of protective sealer, inside and out, and let dry.

3. Cut two strips of the sealed paper that will go all around

53. Inside of octagonal box with decoupage of Pillement chinoiserie shown in Plate 12.

the sides of the box, and also around its lid. Cut them an inch longer than the circumference of the box and lid, and an inch wider than the height (or depth) of the sides of the box and the lid. Cut two more pieces for the top of the lid and the outside bottom of the box. Cut them one-quarter inch longer, all around, than the box measures.

Never cut your patterns the exact size of the box because paper sometimes swells or shrinks. (If it shrinks, you are sunk; tear it all off and start over.) It is far better to have room to maneuver and then trim it to an exact fit after it is glued on.

4. "Butter" one side of the box with all-purpose glue, using your finger to spread it and work it in well. Then dip your finger in water and work that in. One or two dips of your finger in water should be sufficient for one side of a small box. The glue and water mixture should feel like olive oil or melted butter. *Never* try to mix the two together ahead of time. You must allow the heavy glue to "grip" the wood, and then you thin it with water. If you mix it ahead, it will glue down, but it won't stay stuck. This all-purpose glue is peculiar. It will stay stuck for a few hundred years or more if you use it properly. It is completely flexible as long as you keep it moist—not wet. You may pick your paper up and put it down again a dozen times. It won't harm the paper or spoil the finish. You have plenty of leeway—the glue will wait for you.

5. Place your strip of paper (for the side) face down on the table and lay the glued side of the box down on it, allowing about one-half inch of paper to extend from one end about one-quarter inch from the bottom side, and the remaining three-quarters inch from the top edge of the box, as shown in Figure 24. Then start from the end, or rather toward the end of the box, pressing and rolling with your thumb. This is to "set" the paper and stop

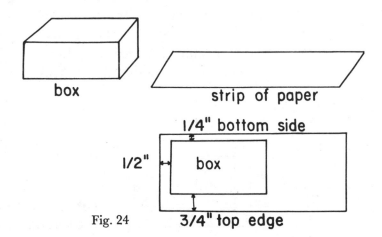

Fig. 24

it from moving or sliding. Now turn the box and paper around and press and roll with your thumb or finger forward. Do not push. It will only stretch the paper and cause wrinkles. Roll, keeping the glue and loose paper ahead of you. What is behind you is glued *down,* not merely on. Again, keep the unpressed glue ahead of you, like a porter with a push broom.

When you reach the end of that side, stop. Glue and water the next side. Roll your paper tightly over the corner, press it firmly so that the corner is sharp and tight, and proceed, rolling and pressing, all around the box. Just before you reach the corner where you started, take the original projecting end and tear it along its end to avoid a sharp line. Fold and glue it around the corner to the last side of the box, coming toward you. Finish gluing that last side right to the end, going right over the overlapped original end. Cut your paper flush with the original corner. This will, or should, leave an invisible seam.

6. Now, trim the *bottom* edge of the box flush with the edge. (Use curved scissors for this, but not your good decoupage scissors. These are *only* for fine cutting of prints.) When I say flush, I mean absolutely flush, and neatly and straightly trimmed, not hacked off and jagged.

7. Then turn the box over and put glue on the top edges. Use no water this time. Rolling and pressing with your finger, work the glue and paper *up* from the sides and *over* the narrow top edge, leaving the corners loose and kind of folded, standing up. These you press together with your two thumbs, thumbnails together,

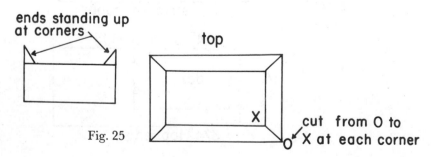

ends standing up at corners

top

Fig. 25

X

cut from O to X at each corner

leaving them standing up but pressed together like rabbit ears at each corner. If all your edges are glued tightly, with no bumps or bubbles of air or glue, take a pair of curved cuticle scissors (again, not your good ones) and cut with the tips from the outside corner of the box to inside corner, Figure 25.

8. Press the now-mitered corners firmly flat with a moist thumbnail and turn and glue the extra paper down on the inside of the box if you are planning to line it with a fabric. If you are planning instead either to paint and/or decoupage the inside, trim it flush with the inside top edge and glue edges down tight. This process is the same for the edges and sides of the lid.

9. Next, butter the bottom of the box with glue and a dab or two of water, and with your finger work it to the same consistency as you did the sides, like oil. Place the paper cut for it on the bottom of the box and, starting from the center, press and fold out to the edges in a widening circle, like a stone dropped into still water.

54. LEFT: *Antique lacquer sewing box; exterior was a ruin, now refinished on ground of madder red over white paper. Decoupage of chinoiserie and Chinese figures and flowers in 18th Century Palette. Interior of original lacquer and pierced ivory. Mrs. James Powers, Needham, Mass.* RIGHT: *Octagonal cigarette box. The "Five Senses of Nature" in Pillement chinoiserie, colored in Sanguine Palette. Inside of lid decoupaged to match, on ground of Venetian green. Mrs. Shepherd Williams, Waban, Mass.*

10. When *all* glue and air bubbles are pressed out, and you have reached all edges, take small curved scissors and trim all the edges flush with the box. Pull both edges, where they meet (sides and bottom), slightly back. Work in a bit of glue and, with a damp thumb and forefinger together to form a wedge, run back and forth along the two edges until they are perfectly together. Let dry. Do not attempt to wipe off all glue immediately. Let it set or it will start to come loose and up again.

11. When the glue is dry, in about a half hour, or the next day (it doesn't matter—the glue is still water-soluble a year later), wring out a piece of ordinary kitchen sponge (cut about one and one-half inches square) in hot water and wipe *along*, not against, the edges, until all glue is gone. Any other dull spots on the paper will also be glue, so remove them the same way. This process also applies to the lid of the box. You are now ready to decoupage it.

HOW TO LINE A BOX WITH PAPER

MATERIALS

Paper cut as per instructions
Protective sealer and brush
All-purpose glue
Bowl of water
1 small piece of sponge
Paper towels

METHOD

1. Prepare your paper according to directions on pages 121-122.
2. Place the box and its lid on the reverse side of the prepared paper and trace the outline of the two pieces as in Figure 26.
3. Measure the thickness of the wood of which the box is made and then mark each side *from the tracing in,* see Figure 27. For example, if the wood of the box is one-quarter inch thick, mark

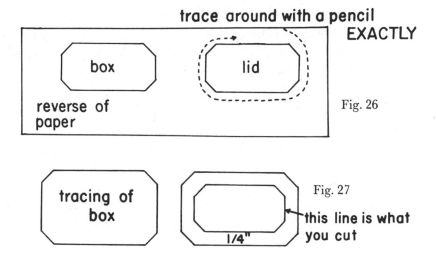

it one-quarter inch smaller on all sides and cut on that marking. It should then fit the inside bottom or top of the box.

4. Now for the sides. Let's say the box is one inch deep inside (from bottom to top edge). Cut a strip that will go all the way around the inside, an inch longer and a quarter of an inch wider, with one edge straight and evenly cut; leave no cut-marks or wobbles. Now you have the bottoms and side strips cut for both box and lid, four pieces in all.

5. Spread all-purpose glue on the inside bottom of the box, working it in with your fingers. Dip your fingers into water; moisten the glue with your wet fingers until it is the consistency of oil. Place the paper cut for the bottom in the bottom of the box. Move it around until it is evenly placed and, starting from the center, work out to the edges, rolling and pressing with the fingers. Don't push, *roll*. Smooth out edges with the flat of your fingernail or any convenient object such as an orangewood stick or a sculptor's wooden modeling tool.

6. When the bottom edges are down tight and smooth, put glue all around the inside sides of the box. Tear off the edge of one end

of your side strip and place it (straight-cut edge to the bottom) at one corner of the box (any corner will do), allowing the torn edge to overlap or go around the corner a bit. Work with fingers or orangewood stick to press it tightly into the corner, then press and roll the paper along the side to the next corner. Get the corner in tight, and go on pasting the next side to the next corner, and so on. Be sure each corner is tight before proceeding to the next side. And please, no round edges, as in the horrible example shown in Figure 28. If you can't get it tight with your finger, use an orange-wood stick. Use anything!

7. When you finally arrive at the last corner (the one at which you started), mark the corner on the paper with your fingernail, pull it back, and cut along the marked line. Reglue to the corner, with the original overlapping piece of torn paper under it. This will leave you with an exact invisible seam. Then trim the top edges of the paper flush with the top edges of the box using your curved scissors. And *voilà!*

8. Allow glue and paper to dry and "set" a bit, then remove any excess glue or glue spots from the box with a small piece of sponge well wrung out in hot water. Never use a wet sponge. Allow to dry, and you may then varnish it or decoupage it.

This technique is used for both the box and its lid.

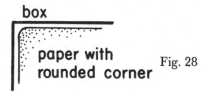

Fig. 28

HOW TO LINE A BOX WITH CLOTH

MATERIALS

Thin white cardboard (the kind that comes in men's shirts or can be bought at a good art store). Be sure it is white, and above all, *thin*.

55. LEFT: *"THE" Williamsburg box, covered in silver tea paper with gold braid on edges. Decoupage of Boucher cupids, etc., all in Grisaille Palette. Central motif on lid is Boucher's "La Musique." By the Mannings; now in the collection of Ruth Hinton Price, Maryville, Mo.* RIGHT: *Hexagonal tea caddy decoupaged in Grisaille Palette on ground of silver tea paper, and designed to accompany "the" Williamsburg box. Inside of lid: cupids and clouds on Venetian flame ground. Designed in Manning Studio; executed by Ruth Hinton Price.*

Cloth (silk, velvet, etc.)
Straight, sharp scissors
Appliqué cloth glue
Bowl of water and paper towels (for clean and dry fingers)
Soft lead pencil for marking
Ruler

METHOD

Cutting Cardboard Liner

Place the box face down on the cardboard and trace carefully around it with a sharp pencil. Subtract the thickness of the wood of which it is made. Mark that, and cut the cardboard on the inside, or subtracted side. Place it in the box. It won't quite fit. Try to figure out which corner or side is causing the problem. Trim it slightly with straight scissors. It probably still won't fit. So put it in, take it out, trimming it each time until it does fit—until when the box is turned upside down it will drop out . . . almost perfect, but loose. Don't ever jam it in. This will cause the cardboard to buckle with tension, and then, no matter how well it is glued down, time and tension will cause something to give, and it won't be the wood.

Next, measure the inside height of the box and lid from its bottom to its top edge. Let's say the inside height or depth of the box is one inch and its lid is one-half inch. Cut two long strips of cardboard, one strip one-inch wide and the other, for the lid, one-half inch wide.

Number each side of the inside of the box (1, 2, 3, 4, etc.). Place a piece of cut strip of cardboard on top of the inside top edge of the box, side number 1. Mark it with a pencil from inside corner to inside corner, and cut. Number it 1 on the back side to match the no. 1 side of the box you measured it for. Proceed, marking, cutting, and numbering each side of the box and cut cardboard. For

56. Interior of "the" Williamsburg box with French trophies, flowers and swags, Boucher cupids, and Abbe St. Non flower wreath on silver tea-paper ground.

example, if the box has four sides, you will have four pieces of cardboard plus the one for the bottom; the same for the lid of the box. Make your number markings on the *back side* of each piece of cardboard, not on the front side. The side that goes next to the box is what is numbered or marked. Do the same for the lid. Now you have ten pieces of cardboard for a four-sided box: two for the top and bottom of the box, eight for the two sides of the box (bottom and lid).

Gluing Fabric to Cardboard

Give all pieces a coat of protective sealer on the front, or unmarked, side. Allow to dry. Spread your silk or fabric face down on the table. Smooth out any wrinkles (or iron it) and place your ten cut cardboards on it, allowing a good half-inch of space around each side of each piece. Place the cardboards so that the grain of the fabric is all going the same way for each piece.

Mark around each piece with a pencil, marking it one-quarter inch wider all around the strip of cardboard.

Using appliqué cloth glue, apply a thin coat to the sealed side of the cardboard, being sure that the entire surface is covered smoothly. Use enough to give you a tacky surface, but not a wet one. Work rather quickly, as this glue dries rapidly.

Meanwhile, rinse your gluey fingers in water and dry, or glue will get all over the cloth. (Glue is water-soluble until dry, but not after.)

Now, when the glued cardboard is tacky, not wet, lay the piece of cardboard, glued side down, on the back side of the material and press just enough to make a firm, light contact. Don't mash it; it will only squash through the material and stain it.

You will have to learn just how much glue to use and how hard to press by trial and error on something you don't care about. It is almost impossible to put down on paper the exact amount of glue for you to use.

Now, when all your pieces of cloth are glued to the cardboards, take the piece for the bottom of the box and trim off excess material flush with the cardboard all the way around. Do not fold it under or it will no longer fit in the box.

For all the side pieces, trim the ends of each piece and the bottom edges flush with the cardboard and leave one-quarter inch of material on the *top* sides of each piece. This you fold over and glue to the back of each piece.

Fitting the Pieces

Now, fit the pieces back into the box. You will find that the material has taken up a bit more space and that you will have to trim each piece again with sharp straight scissors. Cut right through the material *and* the cardboard.

First trim the sides (cutting from the bottom edge) until they are absolutely flush with the top edge of the box or lid, because if they stick up, your box simply will not close when put together. The ends of the cloth-covered cardboards might also have to be trimmed a bit. They must fit evenly at the ends all around the box. Don't trim too much or you will have "gap-o-sis."

Now if it all fits perfectly, take them all out. Apply appliqué cloth glue generously on the bottom of the box. Spread it almost to the edges, but not quite. Put in the cloth-covered cardboard for the bottom and gently press into place with the ball of your finger. Use the tips of your fingers, not your nails, because if the material is satin or velvet it will look scratched.

Do the same with the sides, one by one. A toothpick is handy for application to the sides. But don't get glue drips on the front of the fabric. They will not come off and you'll have to do another one.

Now your box is neatly lined. Do *not* glue in your cloth lining until the box is completely finished—decoupaged, varnished, rubbed down, and waxed—because by the time you have put twenty or more coats of varnish on it, rubbed it down with sandpaper and water, it will be a sorry-looking, unhappy, spotty mess and you'll feel the same. Only glue it in when *all is done!*

This technique should also be followed for the inside of a shadow-box lid, except that you glue it in the lid *first*.

MONTAGE ON A BOX

I said earlier that a montage, a print that's "mounted" in its entirety, occasionally fits into the decoupage family—and we often use a montage on top of a box with decoupage on the sides, or vice versa, or both: Plates 57 and 58. Glue it exactly as you would any decoupage under varnish.

57. Montage of the clipper "Hiram Emery" applied to entire top of dome-lidded box, which is covered in shagreen paper and bound in rope gold braid. Executed by Mrs. Hiram Emery, Providence, R. I. for her son, Hiram Emery, Jr.

58. LEFT: *Montages of Currier & Ives scenes, on top and sides of an old trunk now used as blanket chest. Ground of shagreen paper with blue morning glories and bachelor's buttons. All edges bound in very narrow gold braid.* CENTER: *An old, decoy duck painted Venetian blue with Grisaille decoupage of morning glories and bachelor's buttons.* RIGHT: *Anique tole wood-box. Venetian green borders with decoupage of French trophies; borders and edges bound with gold braid and gold paper ornaments. Trunk and wood-box by Miss Dorothy Simpson, West Newton, Mass.; duck by Mrs. Shepherd Williams.*

 GESSO

Gesso is basically a mixture of bolted whiting, rabbitskin glue, and water. I shall not bother with the exact proportions here, as you can buy ready-prepared gesso in most art stores. But don't buy the kind that has plastic in it. The gesso with plastic is marvelous for sizing canvas, but not for smooth sanding. It is like trying to sand steel.

Gesso for decoupage must be used on new wood only. Its purpose is to hide seams, grainy wood, etc., on furniture, boxes, carvings; or to prepare the piece for gold leafing, for which you need a surface smooth as ivory, to reflect the gold. Basically, it is to cover up the grain of the wood and give an utterly satin-smooth surface to work on in any manner you may wish. (It is the white, chalk-like material seen on a gilded mirror or frame when it has been chipped.)

MATERIALS

    Gesso
    One soft flat ½″ brush
    No. 280-A Wet or dry Tri-m-ite sandpaper, dry
    Steel wool #0000

METHOD

If you are buying ready-made gesso at an art store, buy the dry cold-water gesso. The kind that has to be cooked will ruin your pot, your stove, *and* your disposition, unless you are a dedicated artist immune to such things.

Your gesso, when ready to apply, should be about the consistency

59. *Three colors of gold leaf (pale, lemon, and rich or deep gold) applied on metal, constitute the ground for this large oval tea tray. Decoupage of Pillement chinoiserie figures with borders of motifs taken from the Crown Derby tea service, for which the tray is intended. Crown derby cup and saucer from set show matching border motifs. Jean R. Onwood.*

of heavy cream. Follow directions on the package, but thin it out with more water if necessary until it reaches this consistency.

Now prepare the new raw wood as follows: Make a solution of one-half clear ammonia (not the sudsy kind) and one-half denatured alcohol, mixed together. It smells sneezy, but nice sneezy. This opens the pores of the wood to allow the gesso to "take root" and adhere. Paint the wood with this solution.

Allow the wood to dry, and then apply the gesso as if you were painting with cream. Don't brush it out; flow it on smoothly, avoiding drips and brush marks as much as possible. It is rather like putting a thin, smooth, slick boiled icing on a cake. Allow each coat to dry thoroughly before applying the next one; three to four hours are usually sufficient. If you don't let it dry, it will crack, craze, and buckle, like a dried-up mudhole.

60. *This large desk box, 14" x 12", has a ground of lemon gold leaf, decoupaged with hand-colored prints of Watteau scenes ("Lady in Swing") in tones of lavender, pink, and green. Reverse side of lid also done on lemon gold ground in Watteau manner. Mrs. Shepherd Williams.*

When the last coat is completely dry, sand it as smooth as smooth with No. 280 Wet or dry Tri-m-ite sandpaper (the black, not the red) and sand it dry, not wet. Don't worry if the wood shows through in spots; it's not the look, but the feel, you are after.

Polish it with steel wool #0000 until it feels and almost looks like smooth ivory. Then you are ready either to paint or gild it.

PAINTING ON GESSO

There are two methods for painting:

1. Apply decoupage paint or any paint that has an oil Japan base (see Source of Suppy). Thin by making a mixture that is half paint and half gum turpentine. The gesso will absorb the paint like blotting paper, so you will have to keep applying coats until the surface satisfies you. Allow each coat to dry thoroughly, generally one coat a day, no more. When the last coat is dry, apply a thin, well-brushed-out coat of protective sealer, and your surface is ready for decoupage.

2. Thin protective sealer half and half with denatured alcohol, and apply enough coats of this mixture (allowing each to dry, of course) to the gessoed surface until it finally dries shiny all over. Then apply decoupage paint (see Sources of Supply), or a paint of your choice (but remember, house paint is for houses, *not* for decoupage). Apply as many coats as you feel necessary—generally two are sufficient if properly applied. Then seal it with protective sealer and the surface is ready for decoupage.

Applying Gold Leaf on Gesso

After gesso surface is sanded and steel wool has been used according to instructions, you may apply either oil gold leaf or water gold leaf, and burnish it if desired. You may use a combination of both; on a carving of a frame or on a piece of furniture molding you will water-gild and burnish, while you oil-gild the flat surface. The burnished water gilt method looks like polished gold, like the metal itself. The oil gilt looks matte and soft. This is purely a question of taste. On furniture and frames, and similar items, I like both. On a decoupage box I prefer the oil gilt. But you must make your own choice.

Oil Gilding

Let's take oil gold leaf first. It is simpler but expensive. If the expense dismays you, stop here and skip this whole chapter. Or use metal leaf; it is somewhat cheaper but looks it and eventually turns green (or won't turn green when you want it to). (See section on metal leaf.)

Real gold leaf comes in many grades, colors, and prices, depending on the quality. The five colors are pale, yellow, rich, lemon, and white gold. White looks like silver and will not tarnish as silver leaf will, though that is beautiful, too, if you are prepared for the ultimate blue, tarnished look—I like it. Remember, you get only what you pay for, no more, no less. Let your pocketbook or your conscience be your guide.

These packets of gold leaf may be purchased at most art stores or very fine paint stores. They are not on display, but are usually in the safe, so ask for them. Buy the looseleaf kind, not the kind for glass or for "gilding in the wind," as they sometimes call it; that type is attached to the paper and though it is fine for statehouse domes and signs in windows or on doors, it is not suitable for decoupage.

Before starting on oil gilding, follow the directions on applying gesso. Your gesso should be sanded and smooth and have repeated coats of protective sealer (thinned half with denatured alcohol) until it has dried shiny all over.

Now you may tint the surface if you wish. Your ground is white, but you may also choose several traditional colors: yellow, green, blue, and red. These show through the gold and give it a tone. On a green ground, for example, the gold will take on a greenish tint (lemon gold will help this). On red, it will take on a reddish tint (rich gold will accentuate this). Use yellow gold for a yellow ground, blue under silver, etc. Give the prepared surface *one thin* coat of paint, like a wash. Don't worry about how it looks; it is going to be covered in gold anyway, and is there for tone only, not as a finish. When the paint is dry, give it a coat of protective sealer, and it is ready to gild.

MATERIALS

Patience
A book of gold leaf (again, the loose kind not attached to the paper)
One bottle of Japan gold size (a form of varnish that holds its "tack" for quite awhile)
Two *flat* (not rounded) soft brushes one-half inch wide and one-half inch long (one for gold size, one for gold leaf)
Steady hands and nerves.

Professional or expert gilders will be appalled at this method. Well, this way is for decoupage, not for professional frames and moldings. Their way is fine, but it looks slick, too perfect, and somehow wrong on a varnished decoupage. Actually, the more wrinkled and patchy it is, the better it will look under varnish. Does that cheer you beginners up? A rather crackled, crazed effect is what you are after. And you may feel like that too, after your first attempt.

METHOD

Put a *thin,* well-brushed-out coat of Japan gold size on the top or bottom or one side of the box. Leave the top edges for later. Don't attempt to do everything at once on your first attempt or you *and* the box will end up in a sticky, finger-marked, wasted, gold-leaf mess.

Allow the gold-sized part to dry until it is "tacky"—not wet, but rather like a damp stamp. That is, the varnish is sticky, but does not come off on your finger. Don't mash your finger into it when testing it for tackiness or you'll leave fingerprints. Merely touch it lightly, and when it is tacky you are ready to apply the leaf.

Before you open the gold leaf, see to it that there are no drafts of air in the room. Gold leaf blows away like a dandelion gone to seed. Don't touch it with your fingers—or do try it out once for fun; it will stick to your skin and will not come off onto the box; rub your fingers together, and it's gone!

Now, open your packet of gold leaf. You will find the gold placed loosely between sheets of thin reddish-pink paper. Use this paper to hold and/or touch the gold with; do not use your bare fingers.

Take your second brush (the unused one) and flick it back and forth in your hair behind your ear to the nape of your neck at the hairline. This is to give static electricity to the brush hairs and enable them to attract and hold the gold leaf without pressure. (You must build up this static electricity each time, so don't worry about getting some gold in your hair. When you're finished just run your fingers through your hair and the gold will disappear, I promise.) Apply the flat of the brush gently to the gold leaf. It should jump to it like a pin to a magnet. Don't press, but holding the gold leaf down with the pink paper, partly folded back to expose the gold, touch it with the flat of the brush and gently twist and pull a piece of the gold leaf away. Don't yank it up; pull flatly and gently. A piece about the size of a half dollar is fine. It will be kind of floating on the bottom side of the brush. Gently wave the brush up and down until the piece of gold leaf is level in the air, and in one movement *float* it onto the tacky gold-sized surface. Pull the brush gently away and then lightly, like thistledown, brush it into place. Do not touch the edges of the gold leaf or you will have sticky, tacky goo all over your brush and the gold will stick to that too. To avoid getting into this mess, leave your edges loose for the moment.

Your next piece of gold leaf will overlap a loose edge, and these two edges should be brushed together. But please, use a tender touch. Treat it like a butterfly's wing. Proceed so, over the whole surface, overlapping each piece slightly, like scales on a fish. Do not try to brush off the loose bits of gold leaf in an attempt to be neat. Just let it dry thoroughly, which may take overnight or four days, depending on the weather.

When it is thoroughly dry, polish it and remove loose gold with a small pad of pure silk velvet, but not rayon or cotton, which scratch. (Look in Grandma's sewing kit, raid the attic, or, if all else fails, buy it!) Polish it gently; don't scrub it. Treat it as you would your own eyelid.

You can then proceed to the next side, etc., until you finally reach the top edges of each piece (box and lid), following this same procedure. In time, and with experience, you will be able to do the whole piece at one session.

If, after cleaning and polishing off your loose gold, you find spots that are not covered, take a small pointed brush, dab a bit of the gold size onto it, allow it to get tacky, and patch with a bit of gold leaf. Let dry, and polish off loose ends.

This bit on gold leafing is for those beginners among you who have never even seen a packet of it, let alone used it. I am going into great detail because I don't want any of you to be afraid of it, and because on the first attempt it *is* scary. As for the result looking wrinkled, patched, and blotchy, that is precisely the result I'm after. For after it is decorated with decoupage (covering up a lot of sins) and sunk under twenty or more coats of varnish, it will have a lovely watered-silk or veined look that the perfectly laid gold leaf will never achieve. (Remember, this is for decoupage, not for any other use. It is a background only, not an end result in itself. I quite agree that for an end result it would have to be laid perfectly, the way the experts do it. And when I want to gold leaf a frame, I do it their way.)

Water Gilding

Materials for burnished water gold leaf

Hasting's red burnishing clay (from an art store)
Rabbit-skin glue (art or paint store)
Grain alcohol, *not* denatured (at drug stores; get a doctor's prescription, or sign your life away—and pay, too!)
Agate burnisher (at fine art stores for $4 to $10 and up)
Hot water
A candle warmer or a Salton hot tray
Soft brushes, flat or round (depending on what you plan to gild)
Gold leaf
Two small heat-proof containers, one for the burnishing clay and glue mixture; one for the glue, alcohol, water mixture (both mixtures are applied very warm, not hot)

Water gilding is a devilish process, and if your nerves are shaky and your disposition short, forget the whole thing. It is tedious, maddening, and expensive.

Now only you stalwarts are left to proceed with me on a small venture into what can be hell, or fun, depending on you. But the result *is* beautiful. Besides, think of the money you'll save when little Junior knocks a hunk off a prized antique and you can fix it yourself. (Pay to have it repaired and burnished and you'll find out what I mean, because something is going to suffer—you or your pocketbook, and probably little Junior already has.)

So let's start. Your gesso ground is already sanded and steel-wooled and smooth as smooth and *not* sealed with protective sealer. (Do *not* seal it or you are sunk!) The amount of the mixture in the following directions varies naturally with the size of the piece you

61. *Burnished water gold leaf covers the carvings which adorn this pair of rare Elizabethan consoles, made from our old "Bible table" whose top had split. Of solid oak, painted water green. Decoupage of Adam and Eve by Lucas Cranach. Scrolls and swags from prints of fern spores. Center panel conceals door where the Bible was hidden when the piece was a dining table and Bibles were forbidden! By the Mannings. In author's collection.*

are planning to water gild. I am figuring here on a small box, say six by four inches. We'll start with an acorn, not an oak.

METHOD

1. Take a scant quarter teaspoon of rabbit-skin glue and one ounce of hot water (about three tablespoons) and stir with a small stick, brush stub end, pencil end, orangewood stick, anything you don't care about, until the glue is thoroughly dissolved. If the water steams away, add more to keep it at its original level. When the glue is dissolved, keep the solution warm and put a tablespoon of Hasting's red burnishing clay into the other small heatproof container. Stir, and add enough of the glue and water mixture to it to make it the consistency of heavy cream. You must keep it hot and add glue-water from time to time to keep it flowable.

2. Paint the gesso surface with this mixture. It is red, and, after the first coat, the white will show through a bit. Flow it on

smoothly and hot, avoiding brush marks and drips. When the surface is covered, let it dry for a few hours, then apply the second coat until it is red all over, with no white showing. Allow to dry overnight.

3. Dissolve a very scant quarter teaspoon of rabbit-skin glue again in three-quarters of an ounce of hot water. When it is dissolved, keep it just warm on a Salton tray or candle warmer and add grain alcohol until the mixture turns cloudy and sort of swirls about in the container.

4. Apply this solution to the dried red clay surface. Don't brush it; merely wet it, or the clay will dissolve, being also water-soluble. Allow to dry partially and reapply the mixture. When the surface is wet, float the piece of gold leaf on it with your other dry flat brush. The alcohol will "grab it" and float it flat to the wet surface. Quickly apply another overlapping piece of gold leaf (but for the love of heaven, *don't* brush it, *don't* touch it; it is practically floating on water).

The surface you are to leaf must always be wet with the glue-alcohol-water mixture, but don't, however, allow it to flood back onto the previously applied gold leaf. It makes spots that won't come out or burnish. In other words, keep part of the surface ahead of you wet, so that the laid gold will never touch a dry surface. There must always be an area of wetness around the piece of gold you are laying. If the wet part does not "grab" the gold leaf instantly, you need more alcohol; add it until the mixture clouds and swirls again.

Proceed this way over the entire surface, as it must be finished at one sitting or it will be covered with stop-and-go marks. When you are done (and you *will* be) relax and forget it overnight.

BURNISHING

Next day, if you are still in the running, take your agate burnisher and burnish the gold, using the side or angle of it that is most convenient for you at that particular moment. How do I describe a

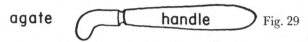

agate   handle   Fig. 29

burnisher? Well, it's sort of like a bent elbow of agate on a wooden handle. It has many surfaces, all rounded, and you use the surface that suits your needs (Figure 29).

When you start to burnish, your gold ground will have a dull look with bits of loose gold flopping around (the overlaps). As you burnish, it will suddenly shine like a bride's wedding ring. Burnish the whole surface, one small area at a time, until it literally glitters like solid, polished gold.

Use medium to light pressure on the gold, rubbing back and forth with the burnisher, not around and around. If you use too heavy a pressure, you will blister it, and bits of gold and red clay will snap off the gesso ground; then, my friend, you've had it. You have to repair that hole from scratch again—red clay, hot pots, and all. So use a medium-light pressure and a certain briskness and wariness. Do not leave any dull or unburnished spots behind you.

When the surface is completely burnished to your satisfaction (it won't be on your first attempt; keep trying), seal it with a thin brushed-out coat of protective sealer, and it is ready to decoupage. Don't forget, I did a dozen bits and pieces before I ever began to be satisfied. I told you it was difficult, nerve-racking, and expensive, so persevere as I did, and you'll eventually get the knack.

APPLYING METAL LEAF ON GESSO

Metal leaf comes in larger sheets and is cheaper than gold leaf. This you may use only on a Japan or oil gold size base. You *cannot* burnish it. You may either lay it with the brush, as in the gold leaf instructions, or with a larger brush, laying the whole sheet, one sheet at a time. Many people can pick it up and lay it with their fingers, like foil. Try any method that is easy for you.

Metal leaf will tarnish in time. Use it if you wish. For decoupage I think metal leaf is a waste of time and effort.

12 ORNAMENTATION AND SPECIAL EFFECTS

MARBLEIZING A SURFACE

MATERIALS

Paint (2 colors)
One soft ½" flat brush
Tissue paper or paper napkins
Turpentine
Rags for wiping off paint if necessary
Protective sealer and brush

Now there is marbleizing and marbleizing. One version turns out looking like the true marble, and *that* is an art in itself.

Then there is marbleizing for decoupage. This must be simple or it will conflict with and overpower your decoupage. (Of course, you may decoupage on an elaborate marbleized ground, but then your design must conform to the ground in a bold way, like the Italian or Florentine "intarsia" method of inlaying stone.)

For marbleizing for decoupage, I use two colors, one light, one dark. I use either a light ground with a darker color for the veining, or a dark ground with a light color for the marbleizing. It's the very simple crumpled paper napkin or Kleenex method. It is not so busy a pattern that it will conflict with a finely cut, elaborately designed decoupage. It merely gives a pleasant mottled background. You are not quite sure what it is, but you know you like it as a base.

METHOD

Let's say you want a red and white marble, with white as the ground and red veinings. First, paint the box or object white, as for a decoupage painted ground. Let dry, and seal with protective sealer and let that dry.

Then take thinned decoupage paint and paint a side red. Crumple up some paper napkins or tissue and lightly dab at the object with the paper while it is still wet. Lift and recrumple the paper, then use a fresh one. Press and lift the crumpled paper until you have the desired effect. Don't wipe.

If you don't like it, wipe it off with a turpentine-dampened tissue and start over, until it does please you. Keep your pattern or veining smallish, as large veinings will look spotty under your decoupage

62. *The Sèvres white ground of this wastebasket is marbleized in pinks, yellows and greens. Decoupage of Pompeian figures, and whimsical touch of Bernini's colonnade split and reversed, give perspective to central figure. Both by Mrs. W. James Moore.*

design. Do the whole piece this way. When done, let dry overnight and then seal it with protective sealer, and you are ready to go.

PINPRICKING

When I speak of pinpricking here it is *not* the complete art of it, but its use in decoupage, as an adjunct to it. I can pinprick with the best of them, but that's not the point here. My method of pinpricking is far from "kosher," but the results for decoupage are! So bear with me, you experts, will you?

It is a system I devised all on my own for decoupage, and it works. I use it solely for decoupage under glass or as part of a collage, and its purpose is to raise a certain part of a print that could not otherwise be raised because it happens to be uncuttable. For *me* to say that is to raise eyebrows across the continent, but, for example, take the coiffure of a Godey lady. You can't cut it out or you'll cut half her head off. The same for a pearl necklace on the same gal, or a tiny series of roses on her décolletage. This method can also be used to make lace look more like lace, or feathers more feathery, etc. (See Plate 93.)

MATERIALS

A rag paper or print with body to the paper
One fine needle; one coarse needle
Handle to attach needle to
Heavy pasteboard to pinprick on
Appliqué glue (or your own)
Toothpicks
Small modeling tool with round ends or that small scoop-shaped thing
that comes in manicure sets

TYPES OF PAPER USED

The first, foremost, and primary thing you need is a print on the proper paper. Magazine paper, glazed paper, thin paper, heavy thick paper *will not do!* The print you plan to pinprick *must* be on medium- to heavy-weight rag, linen, or similar paper that has a soft, almost porous, quality—the kind of paper old prints are done on. I suggest you try a corner of a print, or a similar piece of paper, before you embark on this. The paper has to have what, for want of a better word, I call expansibility; it's texture is soft enough and its fibers are long enough to expand and raise without fraying, fuzzing, cracking, or simply going to pieces.

TYPES OF NEEDLES USED

You can get very elegant and buy yourself all kinds of fancy handles, cork holders, etc., to hold the needles. For myself, I get an old-fashioned penholder, cut a piece of cork to fit in where the nib or pen point would normally go, jam it in tight, and jab the blunt end of the needle into the cork. I bind the whole thing tight with masking tape, and there I have my needle pen! You will need two needles for this, one fine and firm and the other coarser, like a needlepoint or crewelwork needle—but firm!

METHOD

First, select the bits you wish to pinprick on your print—let's say a corsage pinned to a lady's shoulder. It is probably no bigger than the end of a kitchen match, but you want it raised. So, with your fine needle, prick from the front or face of the print, around that corsage, down through the paper, so that when the print is turned over it looks like this from the back (Figure 30, greatly enlarged). The pinpricks are spaced so as not to rip the paper, but are close enough together to give you the outline and form of what you are now going to pinprick and raise. Place your print face down on the pasteboard and, with your fine needle, "pounce" or lightly tap and pound a little bit in from the edges on a diagonal slant, as

Figures of Godey ladies, enlarged (see Plate 93), showing pinpricked effect on flowers on gowns.

shown in Figure 31, *not* straight up and down. Don't try to go through the paper and make holes, but gently pounce and tap with the needle all around the edges and then gradually toward the center, in descending circles, as in Figure 32.

Repeat and repeat, *never* letting the needle go *through* the paper. As the paper begins to kind of loosen or "pulp" and spread, you may lift it a smidgen from the cardboard to allow it to expand until

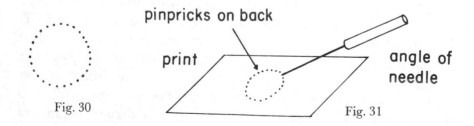

pinpricks on back

print

angle of needle

Fig. 30

Fig. 31

it looks vaguely like Figure 33. Now take your coarse needle and repeat the same process until the print looks like Figure 34.

Then take your spade-shaped tool, a sculptor's modeling tool, or a blunt end of an orangewood stick, anything that will fit the object being raised, and gently, while lifting the paper, press it out and up so that it is raised even more on its right, or face, side. This sort of puts the spread fibers of the paper back together again, so that it now looks like Figure 35.

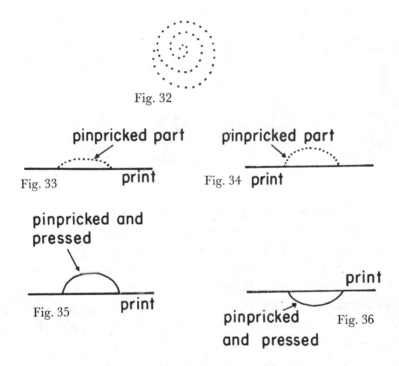

Fig. 32

pinpricked part   pinpricked part

Fig. 33   print   Fig. 34 print

pinpricked and pressed

Fig. 35   print

print

pinpricked   Fig. 36

and pressed

Now give that raised part which is actually placed as in Figure 36, a coat of appliqué glue. Repeat and repeat until that hollow part is filled with glue. Allow to dry, and if the glue is below the surface of the surface, repeat till it dries level with the unpricked paper.

Do this in as many spots and places on the print as you see fit.

You can then cut it out, illuminate it, collage it, or leave it as it is, and frame it.

As my wonderful mother always said to pupils, "Now, *please,* don't bitch it up!" The result can be really amazing, but you *will* feel like a complete moron as you pounce, pounce, pounce and then start all over again. My pupils call it "Idiot's Delight" and love it!

APPLYING MOTHER OF-PEARL

MATERIALS

> Pearl shell
> White vinegar
> Tissue for drying shell
> Bowl of water for rinsing shell
> Appliqué glue
> Foil (if desired)

This is the real, true, natural pearl shell cut to paper thinness (see Sources of Supply), not the thick kind that has to be inlaid into the surface. It can be applied on any surface prepared for decoupage. Its color depends on the color of the surface it is applied to, so place it raw against various grounds to see the different effects it can have. For example, on black it will take on an iridescent bluish purple tone shot with gold; on pink, a rather peach tone. Then there is the method of backing it with foil: gold, silver, or a variety of colors. This gives the pearl shell a bit more of its natural sparkle or *éclat*. But this is a purely personal thing. I shall merely tell you how to cut and glue the pearl shell, how to put foil behind it if you wish to, and how the result should look. You choose the backing.

There are two concepts of working the mother-of-pearl into a design: (1) place and glue the pearl and work the design around it; or (2) design and glue your decoupage with mother-of-pearl in

63. *The Pillement scrolls that form part of this decoupage are inlaid with mother-of-pearl. This small 3' chair screen has an 18th century carved and gilded frame with decoupaged panels on a pale sandy-pink ground with pale Venetian green border. The Mannings. In author's collection.*

mind as part of it. In the latter case, any particular spot or cutting that was planned to have mother-of-pearl under it can then be lifted, the pearl cut for the spot glued down, and then the design reglued on top of it.

I shall use the foil-backed method, because the other is merely the absence of it. I also speak of planning your decoupage for pearl, then lifting the design, inserting the pearl, and regluing. I can't tell you exactly where a piece of pearl goes and what cutting goes around it, so I shall stick to the second method. The first method should come to you automatically.

METHOD

Now to the method with foil-backed pearl. If you are designing the top of a box with scrolls and figures (see Figure 37), place your thin piece of pearl shell, convex side up, on one of the X spots

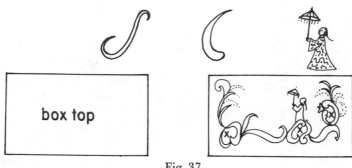

Fig. 37

and with a soft lead pencil trace the outline of the "surround" on the pearl shell.

Put the piece of shell in a small bowl of white vinegar, just enough to cover the pencil-marked area, and leave it there until the stiff shell becomes pliable. Then remove it from the vinegar, rinse it in clean water, and you can cut the shell with small curved scissors. Cut it a bit larger than the pencil-marked area.

Meanwhile, you will have lifted your "surround" of cutting with water, lifted up the two pieces, and dried them and the surface with a tissue.

Cut a piece of foil the exact size and shape of your cut pearl shell and glue it with appliqué glue (shiny side up) to the surface of the box, exactly where you want it. Press it firmly down so that it no longer skids or moves. Then spread the appliqué glue *thickly* on top of the glued foil.

Rinse the vinegar off your softened cut mother-of-pearl in clear water, pat it dry with a tissue, and place it (concave side down, convex side up) on the glued foil. Press it into place with a small, wrung-out, damp sponge. Then rinse the sponge, dampen your fingers on it, and roll and press the pearl into place, rolling from the center of it to the edges as hard and firmly as you can. It won't want to lie flat and will fight back so just be patient and *firm* with it and let it know who is master.

When it is firmly glued and staying put, clean off all excess glue with a damp clean sponge and pat dry with tissue. Then apply all-purpose glue around and over its edges. Reach up and pull your paper cuttings or "surrounds" down onto it. Glue these like any decoupage paper cutting, clean off excess glue, let dry, and there is your mother-of-pearl "inset" into part of the design.

You will be totally disillusioned. The pearl will look flat, dull, dead, with no sheen at all. Don't panic. Just let it dry, finish the rest of your decoupage, clean that all off, and let it dry. Then apply protective sealer as you would for any decoupage under varnish, and there is your mother-of-pearl all shining and glowing again, like pearl should.

Now if you wish to apply pearl to a curved surface, say a chair arm or leg, apply and glue it the same way, only let the pearl shell get a little softer in the vinegar, almost floppy. After you have glued it reasonably and cleaned off all excess glue, wrap two or three loops of string around the pearl and the chair arm to *make* it curve. Tie and wrap it firmly, and let it dry. Then cut the string and there it will be, wrapped around a curve, and it will stay there, too, and look as if it were inlaid.

Remember, the mother-of-pearl can only be cut after it has been softened with vinegar, or it will shatter, chip, and crack. There is another method using boiling water, but the piece remains soft only while *hot* and boiled. The whole process of gluing is the same, but you have to work ten times faster, or spend half the day redunking the pearl shell. The only advantage that I can see is that the pearl remains shiny and brilliant during the whole process. But the end result with vinegar is the same.

ILLUMINATING

MATERIALS

Your print
Colored metallic foils
X-acto knife or razor blade
Decoupage scissors
Piece of glass the size of the print or larger
Appliqué glue

This is a method of allowing hair-thin lines of gold, silver, or other colored foils to shine through the details of a print, and sometimes to show in a glimmer around the edges.

METHOD

Do *not* cut your print out first. Leave it intact. It gives you something to hang onto while cutting. You may use colored prints for this or color your own. In the latter case, they must be sealed first with protective sealer. If you are doing a costume print, for example, decide where you want the foil to glimmer through, say in the fold of a drapery. Put your print on the glass and cut a slit along the side of that fold with your X-acto knife. Then, from the top where you started, cut a hairline of paper out, down to the bottom of your slit. If this is too difficult for you, use your de-

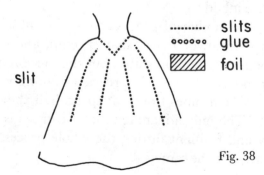

Fig. 38

coupage scissors. Pick up the print and, cutting from the back, pare off a hairline of paper after you have made the slit with your knife. Place it on your foil to get the effect (Figure 38).

You can do as much or as little of this on a print as the spirit moves you. But remember, two different slits must not connect or the piece will just naturally come loose and fall out. Any two slits that are almost converging must have a space of uncut paper between them. Remember that, and it's clear sailing; forget it, and you are on the reefs with a big hole in your bottom and sinking fast.

When your print is cut or slit in as many places as you wish it to be, turn it face down. If you are going to do it all in foil of one color, that's easy. Glue the piece of foil on the back, period! But you might wish to use two or three different colors of foil. Let's use a dress as an example, as in Figure 39.

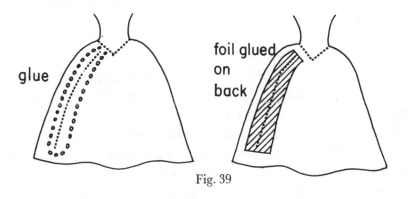

Fig. 39

Glue your foil, bright side down, to the back of the print, slit by slit, using any combination of colored foils which suits you. Turn it face up and check to see that no glue is on the foil showing through the slits. If there is, either pull the foil off and start over with less glue or wrap a toothpick in a bit of damp cotton and swab it off. Don't stain the print, though. (I yank the foil off and do another; it's easier *and* safer.) After everything is illuminated and glued you may cut your print out.

Sometimes you might wish the edges of a print illuminated with foil for an elevated picture, say a flower, butterfly, or bee. That's so simple it is almost idiot's delight. Just whack out a hunk of foil bigger than the flower or bee and glue it on the back of the print, foil or good side down. Turn it over and trim it with your decoupage scissors as fine as you wish. For my own taste, I barely let a hairline of the foil show, so that when it is in a picture you only get a glimmer or a glitter here and there and are not quite sure where it comes from. Understatement is better than overstatement any time.

BURNISHING GOLD POWDER

Gold powder is marvelous for tray painting, stenciling, etc., but *not* for decoupage! It all looks like radiator paint to me, whether in liquid or paste form. Use it if you wish; just follow directions on the packet and good luck.

There is a good type of gold powder on the market and usually available at good art stores called "burnishing gold powder." It is superfine and is used for illuminating and picture mats, etc. I use it for putting touches on gold on figures, scrolls, etc., and I have never known it to tarnish.

Apply it with a very small pointed watercolor brush exactly as you would any watercolor, only—and here is the gimmick— use liquid *gum arabic* instead of water.

Mix a small amount at a time as it dries very quickly. When you are through with the brush, dip it in water to clean, reshape, point and let dry. Then seal your print with glass sealer sprayed on with a mouth sprayer, which you can buy at any art store.

The burnishing powder is sometimes difficult to locate, but it *is* around, so persevere. Though more expensive than the ordinary gold powder, it's worth it and comes in several shades of gold, too.

Gold Braid and Other Ornaments

MATERIALS

Gold braid
Appliqué glue
X-acto knife with *sharp* pointed blade
Fine curved scissors
Tweezers
Small piece of sponge
Bowl of water
Paper towels, tissues
Toothpicks

Gold braid is embossed paper bandings and ornaments (flowers, bowknots, cupids, leaves, etc.) used as narrow bindings on a decoupage piece or as a *tour de force* in itself, such as a box done entirely in interlaced or woven straight braid, or as an elaborate interlaced border on a tray. Again, I think you should either use this in connection with decoupage with great restraint, or else go hog-wild and really create yourself a super *tour de force:* like the little cigarette box with a montage top, set with pearls, and with the sides in interlaced straight gold braid with inserts of mother-of-pearl (see Plate 66); or the gold and peach tray (see Color Plate 3), at which I will *never* make another attempt, although I loved

64. *Paper gold braid insets on tortoiseshell paper ground decorate the new decoupaged bracket for this rare small Louis XIV "cartel" clock; the original wall bracket was missing, and the new gold-braided one matches the clock (which gongs and bongs, too!) Hiram Manning. In author's collection.*

65. LEFT: *The shade of this lamp, made from an old tole tea cannister, is decoupaged with gold braid motifs and with prints from Fort Ticonderoga Continental army soldiers. Miss Dorothy Simpson, West Newton, Mass.* CENTER: *Gold braid boulé work, inlaid with lapis lazuli paper on a ground of gold tea paper, ornaments this shadow box pencil holder; the shadow box bouquet of gold paper flowers is in a mother-of-pearl vase.* RIGHT: *Decoupage of gold paper trellis-work and stars, with Boucher cupids and flowers on a lapis lazuli ground, adorn this tole candy box. Both by Hiram Manning.*

doing it. The gold work alone on that one took six months, two hours a day. Every last bit of that lattice border is cut, quarter-inch by quarter-inch, and placed with tweezers. Unless you have the patience of Job, don't try it. But then again, it can be fascinating, like a jigsaw puzzle: it depends on your temperament.

METHOD

1. Prepare your surface for decoupage as per instructions.
2. Give the gold braid you plan to use a coat of maché varnish on the front side. Don't brush it; lay it on in one swoop of your brush, because if you brush it you are very apt to remove its gold color and wind up with silver braid. When it's dry, do the reverse side. Now you can use it.

I shall concentrate on latticework, weaving, and making a straight piece of braid curve, as the ornaments, flowers, etc., are purely personal taste and are glued down the same way as latticework.

Latticework

For latticework, cut each piece of braid a bit longer than you will need. It gets trimmed to fit *after* it is glued, as in Figure 40.

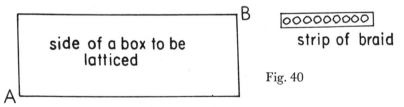

Fig. 40

Spread appliqué glue thinly on the back of the braid with a toothpick and glue it diagonally from corner *A* to corner *B*, letting each end of the braid hang over each end or corner of the box, see Figure 41.

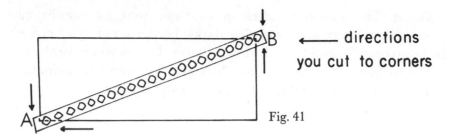

directions
you cut to corners

Fig. 41

Now, take two pieces of braid, one glued and the other not glued to be used as a measurer for spacing. (You can use it later at the end for the corners and small bits.)

Lay the unglued piece of braid next to and abutting the previously glued piece. Place the glued strip of braid next to that, press it into place, remove the unglued strip, and trim the edges of the second glued strip as you trimmed the first one, see Figure 42. Proceed thus until you have reached the corner of that side of the box. Then repeat from your original strip up to the other (or top) corner. Your box or side will now look like this, see Figure 43.

Now, with *hot* clean water and a damp, wrung-out piece of sponge, remove any and all traces of glue. Let dry.

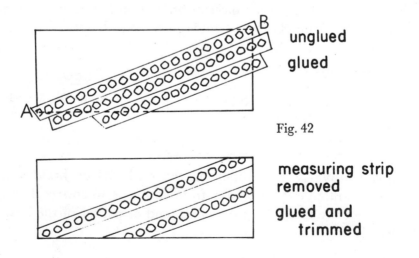

unglued
glued

Fig. 42

measuring strip
removed

glued and
    trimmed

Then we come to the nasty bit of lacing the gold braid back across the diagonals, in the exact opposite direction, from C to D. So drag out the *sharp* knife, steady your nerves and hand, and we'll proceed. I'm going to call the original diagonals of braid *strips 1* and the second diagonals coming from C to D *strips 2*. Then I will number each strip from C to D: 1, 2, 3, 4, 5, 6, 7, as in Figure 44.

Now glue strip 2 from *C* to *D* in the direction, of *D, over* 1, and when you reach 2, cut it with your knife *on* and abutting 2, and on the opposite side of 2 also, so that it seems to run *under* 2. Glue it over 3, cut on both sides of 4, over 5, under 6, over 7. It will now look like Figure 45.

Lay your unglued strip of braid next to strip 2. Lay your glued strip next to that, remove the unglued strip, and cut the second glued strip the opposite of the first strip. In other words, strip 2

66. *Pair of hexagonal tea caddies; Pillement chinoiserie on green gold-leaf ground.* CENTER: *This richly adorned cigarette box, done in the Fabergé manner, has sides decoupaged with basket-weave gold braid and gold paper cartouches inset with mother-of-pearl. Lid is a montage of a Venetian scene by Canaletto, with border of seed pearls. Hiram Manning. In author's collection.*

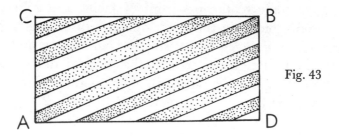

Fig. 43

went over 1 and under 2, so glue and cut your second glued strip
under 1 and *over* 2, under 3, over 4, under 5, over 6, under 7, as in
Figure 46.

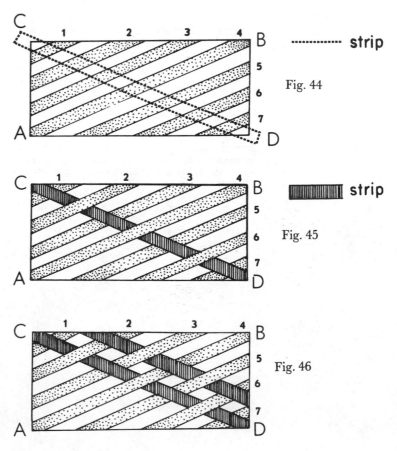

‑‑‑‑‑‑‑‑‑‑‑‑ strip

Fig. 44

‖‖‖‖‖‖‖‖ strip

Fig. 45

Fig. 46

Proceed this way up to corner B, then start from the center strip and go down to corner A. Mop any excess glue off with hot water and a damp sponge and let dry. You will now have an interlaced, or latticework, effect.

Weaving

The weaving effect is achieved by the same method, except there are *no* spaces left between the pieces of gold braid. It is solid, one piece next to the other, as in Figure 47.

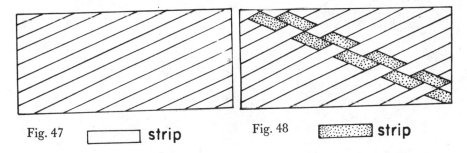

Fig. 47   **strip**   Fig. 48   **strip**

After the entire piece is covered in this manner, the edges may be bound or "edged" in gold braid, to give the effect shown in Figure 48.

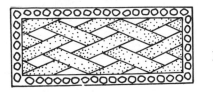

Fig. 49

The top and bottom pieces of gold braid are glued and run all the way around the top and bottom of the box, with extra braid allowed to pinch both ends together at one corner. The braid is cut with scissors, and glued down for an invisible seam. The upright corner pieces are glued together to meet on the corner. They are cut with the knife after they are glued to fit between the top and

67. *Bits of gold braid by the thousand form the basket-weave border of small serving tray, 14″ x 18″, decoupaged in the Sevres porcelain manner, after author's large gold tray. Center oval of gold braid interlaced with hand-colored flowers; border medallions of gold paper on mother-of-pearl ground, with lattice and star gold paper overlay. By Frances D. Cross.*

bottom edges (if you still have your sanity left and your bifocals still fit).

Making a straight piece of gold braid curve

To make a straight piece of gold braid curve, there are two methods, depending on the braid. For solid straight-edged braid with no lacy or cutout innards, as in Figure 49, take your fine scissors or knife and nick the edges on both sides, as in Figure 50.

Each nick on each side alternates so that the braid is *not* cut through. You can then glue the back with appliqué glue and curve it, as in Figure 51. Of course, this is an exaggerated drawing, merely to demonstrate the idea to you. Actually, the nicks would be so small as to be all but invisible.

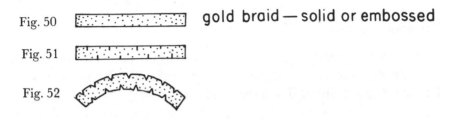

Fig. 50   gold braid — solid or embossed

Fig. 51

Fig. 52

For an elaborate braid with a pierced or laced interior, there is a bit more cutting involved, as in Figure 52.

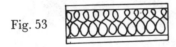

Fig. 53

With your fine-bladed scissors, cut off the two outer straight edges. Glue one straight edge in a curve, see Figure 53.

Then add the center and glue it next to the first glued edge, as in Figure 54.

Then glue the second straight edge to the bottom of the center edge, see Figure 55.

There is your curved braid, intact, and no one knows how you did it except you, the glue pot, and a few raveled nerves. But remember, this is precision work, and if it is not cut straight and glued straight, it is not going to look straight.

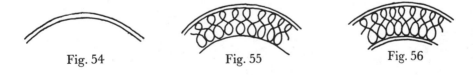

Fig. 54   Fig. 55   Fig. 56

Also remember that gold braid, since it is embossed and a double- or triple-thickness of regular prints used in decoupage, is going to require just that much more varnish: twenty coats of varnish minimum for regular decoupage, and at least ten extra coats for each thickness of gold braid. *Ergo,* interlacing involves two thicknesses of gold braid, so twenty more coats of varnish.

Turning gold braid to silver

If you want to turn gold braid to silver, wet a piece of cotton with nail-polish remover or lacquer thinner and wipe the braid with it. Presto! Instant silver! Then seal and use.

Le Goût

13 PAPER-MACHE COLLAGE

MATERIALS

All-purpose glue and appliqué glue
Facial tissues, paper towels, waxed paper, newspaper, cardboard
An electric blender
A cereal bowl and water
A tough old kitchen teaspoon
Sculptor's wood modeling tool with rounded edges
A small piece of sponge
X-acto knife, with straight sharp pointed blade
Flat toothpicks, tweezers, spatula
Protective sealer, and soft flat half-inch brush
Varnish, and soft flat half-inch brush
Matte final finish, and brush
Plain white typewriter paper
Colored pencils or colored foil
Spackle paste

WHAT IT IS

Paper-mache collage is a method of taking a flat print, a figure, a flower, etc. and actually modeling it on a paper-mache filling until it has a third dimension, like a bas-relief. The flat print takes on a sculptured look.

When this form of decoupage is used with taste and restraint, it is truly beautiful! Overdone and overblown, it can descend to the very worst of Victoriana.

There are two basic uses for paper-mache collage. The version which is easier to use goes under glass, for pictures, shadow boxes etc., and we discuss it first. Later in this chapter, under "Collage to Use on An Outside Surface," we cover the more difficult version.

THE BACKGROUND

Collage under glass is used in shadow box frames or frames with at least one inch between the backing and the glass. You can do a figure or a group of them on almost any background: silk, satin, moiré, velvet, a painted ground or a paper ground—though I think paper or paint is a bit harsh. Silk, velvet and cloth are kinder. I think you will prefer fabric for a flower picture in the eighteenth-century manner or a modern arrangement. I have done several black-and-white flower arrangements on heavy white linen and the results were smashing!

Let us work with a figure first, and then do the flowers.

PREPARING THE PRINT OF A LADY FOR FILLING

Take a figure that has been cut out and colored. With a sharp X-acto knife cut and raise certain details of the costume or body: hands that are resting on a dress, for example. Cut out the piece you want to raise by cutting around its outline. For example, a hand and arm resting on a dress, Fig. 56. Cut from X1 around the arm and hand back up to X2, but do not go to the edge of the dress or the arm may get cut off and a gaping hole will be left. Do the same with a flounce or ruffle, Fig. 57. Cut from X1 to X2, but do

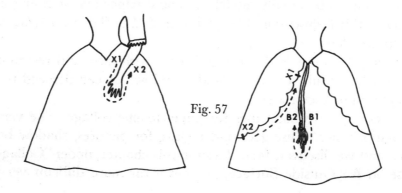

Fig. 57

68. *Collage of fruit and berries. Large fruits collaged on paper-mache base; berries and leaves backed with glue and hollow-molded. Yellow satin ground, in gold leaf frame. Mrs. Clara Friedman.*

not cut to the edge. Do the same with the tassel on the dress. Cut from B1 to B2, leaving the tassel still attached to the dress, but loose and capable of being raised to give it dimension.

PREPARING A FLOWER PRINT FOR FILLING

With flowers the same principle applies:

Cut around petal X, but do not cut it from the back to the center A, or it will fall off. Leave a bit of paper between A and X before you start, and stop short of A when ending. This way petal X can be raised and still remain attached to center A, see Figure 58.

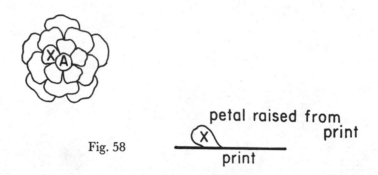

Fig. 58

petal raised from print

print

If you are confused at this point, go back and re-read the last few paragraphs. Cut a few pieces you don't particularly care about and practice with them. This is a particularly difficult step to communicate. To repeat: Cut out the particular detail with the knife in order to partly lift it, but still leave it attached to the main body of the print.

When you have mastered this part, the next step is to back the print either with colored foil (gold, silver, pink, blue, etc.) or color a piece of plain paper with your colored pencils to match the pieces you have cut to elevate. The print is backed to prevent the paper-mache from oozing through these cuts. Foil is simple... just choose the color you want and use it. But if you are using colored paper—say you are doing a pink rose which has been cut and had its petals elevated—do this: Take a thin piece of white paper and color it with colored pencils the color of the deepest part of that rose. The piece of paper must be the size of the rose (or whatever you happen to be working on.)

The petals you have partly cut to elevate we will call the *loose* part, and the part that is not cut, the part the petals are attached to, we will call the *solid* part. Turn the print over, face-down and, with a toothpick, apply appliqué glue to the solid part, but not so much that it will ooze out onto the loose part. Place your piece of colored paper (or foil) face down on the glued print and press it into place. Turn it over and with your tweezers lift each of those loose parts to make sure they have no glue on them. Trim off any edges of paper that might show around the outside edges of the piece. Let it dry, then it will be ready for the paper-mache.

PREPARING THE PAPER-MACHE

You will use tissue paper and the electric blender. For safety's sake, never put your hand in the blender jar when the blender is turned on, or while the jar is still on its base.

1. Separate the tissue into two sheets, and put them under the blade separately. The tissues are two-ply, and are easily separated. Put the blender back on its base, cap it, turn it on, and a moment or two later, turn it off. You should have what looks like fluffy raw cotton.

2. Remove blender from base, and transfer the fluffed tissue to a bowl. Put more tissue under the blades, and repeat the process of blending until your tissue fills the cereal bowl. The amount of tissue you need depends on the size of the piece you collage. A cereal bowlful is just about enough for a large rose, so judge the other pieces accordingly.

3. To the tissue in the cereal bowl add almost a half jar of all-purpose glue. Mix, mash and stir it up with your tough old spoon until it looks rather like a raw codfish cake, with no white lumps of tissue. Remove anything that does not blend in.

FILLING THE FLOWER PRINT

1. Place your prepared print face down on the table and with a spoon plop on some of the prepared paper-mache. Let's assume you are filling a life-sized large double rose. The mixture should be about half-an-inch thick in the center, tapering down to the edges, like an upside-down saucer.

2. Cut a sheet of waxed paper about twice as big as the rose. Pick up the rose, filled with paper-mache, and turn it onto the wax paper, right side up.

3. Lay two or three layers of facial tissue over the rose. Wet the tissue down thoroughly with a sopping wet sponge, until the tissue is transparent and clings to the rose so that you can see the flower through it. Let it stay that way for at least a half hour to three-quarters of an hour. If it starts to dry, wet it again. This makes the paper rose malleable for sculpting, and is a process that cannot be hurried.

4. After half an hour, test the print with your finger or modeling tool to see if it is pliable and does not craze or crack when you attempt to mold or shape it. If it is ready and pliable, remove the wet tissue and, with your fingers and wood modeling tool, begin to mold or shape it as follows: First press down and indent the center with your finger which will cause the paper-mache to rise underneath the flower petals. From the center radiate out like spokes of a wheel with the modeling tool (only not that mechanically) to mark the petals. To form them, hold (do not press) the part you wish to go down with the modeling tool and push the paper-mache toward it from the top with your fingers so that the paper rises up where you want three-dimensional fullness.

5. Never push with your modeling tool. You will only poke holes in the paper and ruin it. This step may take some practice until you get the feel and form of it. Remember, hold with the modeling tool; push with the fingers.

6. As you work, remove any paper-mache filling that may be oozing from the sides or edges. Pull it away with the modeling

69. *Paper-mache collage bouquet of Grisaille flowers, green ferns, gilded paper basket, and butterflies set with mother-of-pearl, on* bois de rose *silk ground. Designed by Maybelle Manning; executed by Mrs. Everett L. Cuneo.*

tool or tweezers, or poke it back under with your fingers.

7. With a spatula, gently transfer the modeled rose from the waxed paper to a layer of newspaper. Nick and cut the edges of the newspaper to prevent them from curling up around the sculpted flower when they are baked.

FILLING THE LADY PRINT

1. Follow the directions given above under "Filling the Flower Print". Using the modeling tool, hold the figure and mache as directed and pushing with the fingers, depress her neck, push out her head and chest and push in her waistline. The folds of her dress will vary, depending on where you want fullness; some folds will be in, some out.

2. When this is done, pull the "loose" pieces of the print away with the tweezers so that they stand elevated, straight up in the air.

3. Clean the print and transfer to newspaper, as directed in steps 6 and 7 above. Now bake, and finish the elevated or loose pieces as directed below.

BAKING THE PAPER-MACHE

Place the molded print and the newspaper on a piece of cardboard and put it in a slow oven, 140 to 150 degrees F. Let it bake for approximately one-and-a-half hours, with the oven door open or closed, depending on your stove. Remove it from the oven and let it partially dry. Pull the newspaper away from the bottom, and with strong curved scissors remove any bits and pieces of paper-mache that may show. With a damp sponge remove any glue or particles from the top of the print. Let it dry if it is for under glass; if it is intended for the top of a surface, now is the time to apply the finish.

FINISHING THE LOOSE PIECES

While the piece is drying, for under glass, you can finish doing your elevated or loose pieces. (So far you have worked on the solid part.) Lift them up with fingers or tweezers and give them a *thin* coat of appliqué glue. Let dry, and with your tweezers and fingers, shape, bend and twist them into the shape and form you want.

When the piece is thoroughly dry and hard as cement, tint the elevated edges that might show with wet, colored pencils or water-colors to match that part of the piece: pink rose edge, pink; blue dress, blue, etc. Then give it a coat of protective sealer, front and back, and let it dry. Next, give it one coat of varnish, front and back, and let that dry. Finally, give the front side a coat of matte final finish; let that dry. The paper-mache flower or figure can now be framed alone or used as part of your composition. In Plate 70 dozens of the paper-mached pieces have been combined.

GENERAL ADVICE

1. Every flower or figure that you plan to use in a picture does not have to be modeled and elevated as described here. Some may simply be molded or collaged without elevating what we have called the loose bits. Other parts of your composition are left per-fectly flat and worked into the whole.

2. On all of the flat pieces, first apply thin coat of appliqué glue to the back to prevent them from curling up, as paper tends to do in time. They may also be lightly shaped and formed with tweezers and fingers, and will remain that way when coated on the back with glue, even after they are in the picture, framed and hung.

The mechanics of raising one flower over the other and gluing in your flat pieces (leaves, ferns, etc.) are covered under "Shadow Boxes, *Vue d'Optiques* or Elevations."

Pinpricking may also be used in combination with this process, if you wish. The pinpricking is done *before* it is molded (see "Pin-pricking").

COLLAGE TO USE ON AN OUTSIDE SURFACE (NOT UNDER GLASS)

This has a carved or repoussé look. Select a background for it as discussed earlier in this chapter. Now cut out the print to make a

solid section, but do not raise any "loose" pieces with your knife.
The piece is molded only.

Prepare the paper-mache mixture exactly as described earlier in

70. *Paper-mache collage picture, 4′ x 4′. Collage of Redouté roses; miscellaneous
flowers; Gould's tropical birds with mother-of-pearl beaks; elevated and shaped butterflies. Design by Maybelle Manning; executed by Mrs. William Gillespie, Syracuse,
N.Y.* TECHNIQUE DETAILS: *butterflies: some backed with foil, then cut back so foil
shows as illumination; some with mother-of-pearl. Flowers: some backed with foil;
some have petals raised and collaged with paper-mache. Leaves: some molded; some
simply shaped; some flat.*

71. Dining-room screen, 7'. Large birds are collaged with paper-mache, and have mother-of-pearl beaks and eyes, on background of squares of gold tea paper, all under varnish. Mrs. Kimball Powning.

this chapter, but mold it so that all the edges are turned down or molded to the background, leaving no edges standing up. This is important, for otherwise it won't glue down properly on the outside surface. Your collage should look as if it were carved from its background, and loose paper edges will spoil the effect.

After the collage is molded, bake and clean as directed, trimming any bits of paper-mache from the edges. Let the piece dry until semi-hard, not bone-hard as you would for under glass. The edges must still be pliable.

Now glue the piece onto your prepared surface with appliqué glue. Firmly press down the collaged piece and all edges, cleaning up with a damp sponge any glue that oozes out. Put a weight on it (I use old flatirons) and let it dry.

When it is dry, check all the edges, and if there are any that are not flush with the surface, they can be filled in with a little Spackle paste and painted to match the surface.

Apply varnish, pulling it out from any hollows and away from where it joins the surface so as not to have gummy puddles.

Sand, following naturally the contours of the collaged print. Be careful in sanding the top, or elevated, parts. Do the bottom parts first, then the tops. If you sand through the paper to the paper-mache underneath, don't bother looking up "Pitfalls, Disasters, and Their Cure" because for that the Doctor is out!

14 DECOUPAGE ON SILK

Silk makes a beautiful lining for a box, a picture under glass, or a silk lampshade, bellpull, etc.

MATERIALS

Silk (taffeta, satin, etc., but not velvet)
Appliqué cloth glue (or glue of your choice).
Thin white cardboard for a box, heavier cardboard for a picture.
Straight scissors (to cut the cardboard and silk).

Bowl of water.
Flat toothpicks.
Tissues and paper towels.

If you plan to line a box, look up "How to Line a Box with Silk." After lining, you may proceed as below to apply the design to silk. For a picture, instead of cutting three edges flush and folding one edge over, as for lining a box, fold all the edges over and glue them to the back of the cardboard.

72. *This magnificent 17th century "cavalcade" is a paper-mache collage, done in Full Palette on red velvet ground. Mrs. Stephen L. French.*

73. *The decoupage of pink roses, blue forget-me-nots and golden yellow scrolls is glued directly to the ground of pale blue silk faille in the interior of this shadow box. The silk is not varnished, nor need it be. (See Plate 88 for outside view.)*

74. *These Raphael prints in 18th Century Palette are elevated over a shot silk ground pale blue; the gold leaf frame, 3'6", has a border of apricot velvet. Hiram Manning. In author's collection.*

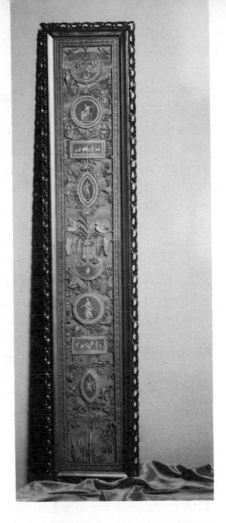

METHOD

If your silk is glued to the cardboard and your cuttings are ready, place your design of cuttings on the silk, unglued, exactly where you want it. Lift a corner of the cutting here and there and make a mark on the silk under the edge of the print with a pencil. This is to enable you to lift the print away to apply the glue and to have a guide to replace it in that exact spot. Before you start to glue the cutting to the silk, remember that once you have glued it, you cannot move it. If glue oozes out from the edges of the cutting onto the silk, it will spot.

With a toothpick dipped in appliqué glue, spread the glue thinly in the middle of the print. Place the print on the silk and press it into position. Pull one side or part of the unglued cutting up and back until you reach the glued part, then put glue on the unglued part thinly and press that down. When you approach the edges of any cutting, apply a very thin coat of glue with your toothpick. Lightly wipe off any excess and press the print gently into place with a clean dry tissue. This will help absorb any glue that might ooze out and spot the silk. Glue this way, tendril by tendril, leaf by leaf, stem by stem, working from the center of the print outward. It is better to put too little glue on and reglue it than to spot your silk, because in that case you only have three choices: live with it; add a leaf or something to cover the spot; or do it all over.

When you think everything is down tight and there are no more spots, leave your work for a half hour. Then check for loose cuttings by running your fingernail lightly against the edges of your cuttings and reglue if necessary. When it is dry, it is finished. You can then glue it in your box, frame it, or use it as you wish. I have a short answer to a frequently asked question, "You mean you don't varnish it or anything?" . . . "No, you don't!"

SILK LAMPSHADES

The technique for silk lampshades is basically the same. Hold a cardboard behind the side of the silk shade you are decoupaging to give you something to press against. Glue the design to the shade, remove the cardboard, and the design is placed. The heat from the light bulb will not affect the glue. To clean, dust as you would any silk shade.

15 DECOUPAGE UNDER GLASS—LAMPS AND PICTURES

"Under glass" includes first, lamps, and, second, pictures which are actually glued to the underside of the glass. Anything else will

75. *Pair of large lamps, 19" high. Sèvres white ground with decoupage of Pillement chinoiserie in blue Toile de Jouy Palette. Maybelle Manning. In author's collection.*

be under its own category, such as shadow boxes, *vue d'optiques,* montages, collages, etc. For pictures, you need the glass, its frame, and its backing—cardboard or wood. I prefer wood, as it gives more protection to the glass. For lamps, you need the piece itself, hurricane globes, cylinders, lamp chimneys, anything of that nature that forms the base of your lamp. It has to be clear glass, and you have to be able to get your hand inside with working room to spare, otherwise you'll end up like the little boy with his hand in the candy jar: he can't get it out without letting go of the candy. You have to maneuver all those designs and cuttings in there, so leave yourself room!

MATERIALS

> Your glass piece (lamp, or a sheet of glass with a piece of cardboard or wood cut to the same size)
> The cuttings you plan to use, colored and cut
> All-purpose glue
> Bowl of water
> Small piece of sponge; facial tissues or paper towels
> Glass sealer
> Four brushes: two half-inch, soft, flat brushes for protective sealer and varnish; one quarter-inch brush for paint or opaline; and one small pointed watercolor brush for glass sealer
> Your ground (paint, opaline, gold leaf, whatever you plan to use)
> Aluminum foil (the kitchen kind, but thin)
> Protective sealer (for the background)
> Varnish
> Small curved scissors
> X-acto knife or razor blade

LAMPS: PREPARATION AND APPLYING DECOUPAGE

METHOD

1. You have your cuttings, colored and cut. (Sealing is optional: prints under glass don't need it, but the sealer does give more

body and makes the cutting easier.) First of all, place them to one side, each piece of cutting separate, colored side up. This is to make them easily available when you search for that particular flower or figure with wet fingers. Have your glass lamp base in front of you, and glue, water, sponge, etc., at hand.

2. Pick your central motif first. Lay it on the outside of the glass to see about where you want it and how much area of glass you will have to butter with glue, allowing room to spare. Put the cutting aside.

3. Now dip your finger or fingers in all-purpose glue and spread it on the inside of the glass, where the cutting is to go. Dip your fingers in water, and work the water with the glue inside the glass till it feels like melted butter or oil. If it separates inside the glass base, you have too much water; add more glue. When it is the consistency I've mentioned, dip your fingers in water to remove the glue, and remove any excess water from your hands with a damp sponge.

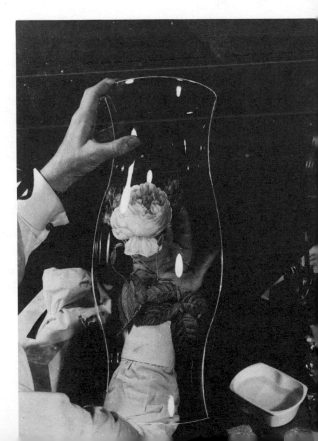

76. *How to glue under glass. Glass and print are facing you while your hand presses glue and air out from between print and glass. Press from center outward to edge of print. Don't forget the damp clean sponge and water shown at lower right.*

4. Take your cutting or central motif and slip it inside the lamp base, face toward the glass. Move it around—up, down, left, right —till it is in the *exact* position you want it. I don't mean hold it away from the glued surface; I mean put it onto the glue and slide it around right in it. When it is where you want it, take your damp wrung-out piece of sponge and tamp the cutting firmly into place, flat against the back or inside of the glass.

5. Wring your sponge out so it is clean, and if your fingers are sticky rinse them and damp-dry them too. Then, keeping your fingers constantly clean and damp, roll and press with your fingers from the center of the design out to its edges. This is a kind of backward process because the glass base is resting on the table, supported by your left hand. Your right hand is inside the glass. The print is facing you, and your hand and fingers are behind the print pressing the glue out. You have to do it this way, because you can see the glue and air bubbles move on the surface of the print through the glass. You want to get every last one of the little stinkers *out* to the edge of the print and then *off*, away, gone! (Plate 75.)

6. When that is done, run the damp flat of a fingernail around the edges, pressing from the paper toward the glass. Make sure that every last edge of leaf, tendril, or ribbon is down firmly and *tight*, or you are in for trouble later; like when you paint it, and the paint runs into that nice inviting loose edge and makes a mess of what you have glued on (again I refer you to "Pitfalls, Disasters, and Their Cure"). You can proceed so, around the whole glass base, applying bits and pieces of cutting as it pleases you, getting each one tight and firmly down as you go.

7. If at any point you wish to glue something on—leaf, figure, flower, whatever—and the surface has half-dried glue on it, moisten it with a wet finger and rub around till the glue is once more oily. Add a bit more glue to be sure, and go on designing.

8. If at any point in your gluing and designing you decide you don't like that particular bit where it is, wet it, give it a chance to

come loose, and take it off. Rinse and dry it and put it aside for further use. Reglue the surface and any adjoining loose bits and glue on the cutting you do want. Don't forget, with all-purpose glue you stick it where you want it, but you aren't stuck with it. So relax, and design.

9. Sometimes a print or cutting gets contrary, particularly on a curved glass surface, and it *will not* do what you want it to do. If it is still moist, pull it away from the glass, nick it with your scissors, add more glue, and push and prod it with your fingers, scissors' points, anything, till it does what you want it to. Again, a largish piece will adhere at the sides, but pull away in the middle. So lift or soak one side loose, poke glue and a dab of water in there, and with a damp sponge wrung out in *hot* water, "sweat" it on (a term used by many craftsmen to describe how to make a thing do what it won't or doesn't want to do). The hot damp sponge will allow the paper to expand just enough so that it *does* have room to adhere to that curved surface.

10. Now, when every last bit of your design is glued down tight, wipe off excess glue on the clean or blank surfaces only and let the poor thing dry completely and compose itself overnight.

11. Next day, or whenever you feel like it, use your damp sponge wrung out in *hot* water and, pulling from the edge of each paper bit toward the clear glass, remove every last ounce of glue. Your glass must sparkle! But don't use glass cleaner; use water only! If any bits come loose during this mopping up, reglue them at once and continue cleaning. Never get it wet or it will all come off; just have it damp. When everything is clean and still glued down tight, give it a nap. Let it dry!

12. Then take your glass sealer and with your small pointed brush run around *every* edge of your decoupage design with it. Run your brush partly on the paper, partly on the glass, just enough so that the paper edge and the glass surface are sealed together. Let that dry.

GROUNDS

Now you are ready to apply your background or ground. There are so many grounds to back your decoupage lamp with, I hardly know where to begin. So I think I had better try to divide them into basic categories, describe a few, and leave the infinite variations up to you.

Basically, you have a ground: paint, opaline, paper (tea, marbleized, etc.), foil (metallic), leaf (gold, silver, etc.), powder (gold, silver, blue, green, any color it comes in).

Remember, your ground has got to be opaque, or you'll be able to see the inner workings of the lamp (wiring, etc.) from the outside. So unless you are using paper or foil as your ground, you must combine *two* grounds: i.e., paint, opaline, leaf and powder must be backed by foil. Clear?

Paints

Let's take them in the order named, and start with paint. Under glass your paint will not change color as it would under varnish, so pick the color you want. The only paints I can personally recommend, outside of my own which was designed for this purpose (see Sources of Supply), are paints on oil Japan base. They have enough body not to run and crawl under the edges of the paper and they will permanently adhere to the glass. There are doubtless other paints equally good, but I know that my paints and Japan-base paints stay put. From sad experience, however, I do know that *some* won't work.

I will tell you how to apply the paint that I know works. You want your paint neither thick nor thin, but thin is the lesser evil. Stir your paint thoroughly and see that there are no lumps or scum in it. To start with, use a quarter-inch, flat, soft brush. Dip it in the paint and wipe it off on both sides on the lip of the paint jar to remove excess paint. You want a rather dry brush to start with to avoid "rununders," as I call them, which can occur in spite of the glass sealer.

Hold your lamp with the design up and facing you. Put your brush inside the lamp and apply the paint to the edges of the design, pulling the paint out a bit onto the glass. (You don't need to paint the backs of your print or cuttings.) When all the edges are painted this way, you can fill in the open spaces of plain glass, as follows:

Start in the middle of the lamp and go ring-around-the-rosy, doing your edges with a dry brush and filling in the open spaces with a fuller brush. Gradually come down to one end of the lamp in descending circles and then reverse, from the middle down in circles to the other end. The reason I tell you to do it this way is that otherwise you, your sleeves, etc., are going to be covered all over with paint. Don't worry about brush strokes; they all disappear with the next coat. If they don't, you'll need a third coat. Allow each coat to dry thoroughly before applying the next.

When the paint is dry, line the lamp with florist's foil, with the plain silver side of the foil (if colored) facing the painted surface to make the surface completely opaque. Tear the foil into rounded pieces about the size of a fifty-cent piece or a bit larger for easier gluing: large pieces won't conform. You'll need a pile of them. You should begin with a ring of them around the inside center, as you did with your paint. Put a thin film of all-purpose glue (with no water this time) on the plain side of the foil and glue it to the inside of the lamp, on the painted surface, using a damp finger to get it down tight. Put glue on the next piece and put that next to the first piece, overlapping slightly, like fish scales. Cover the whole inside of the lamp this way, being sure that each piece is down tight. Trim the top and bottom edges flush with the rim of the glass with a razor blade or X-acto knife, and reglue them *tight*. Clean off any excess glue with a clean damp sponge and allow it to dry.

Then apply a very thin coat of protective sealer, using a half-inch soft brush, and let that dry. Finally apply two coats of varnish, one coat a day, making sure the edges of the rims are varnished too. Clean up the outside, and your lamp is ready for its base, cap, and wiring.

Opaline

Opaline is a liquid on a lacquer base that has a pearl-like quality. An extremely beautiful background for a lamp, it can be backed with various colored foils to tone it or to allow bits of the foil to glimmer through here and there. It is applied practically the same way as paint.

Your decoupage is designed, cleaned, dried, and sealed with glass sealer. Stir the opaline up, don't shake it, and with a small pointed brush go around the edges of the cuttings, pulling the opaline away from the paper toward the glass. Then, with a quarter-inch flat brush, using more opaline this time, swirl it around with your brush to achieve an uneven, pearl, cloud-like appearance. Ever rolled a pencil between your thumb and forefinger? Roll the opaline brush that way, pressing the brush against the glass. When the desired effect is achieved, let it dry. No sealer is needed.

Colored Foils

Colored foils are cut and applied the same way as described above with aluminum foil. Take a piece of colored foil and hold it inside the lamp to see if you want that much foil to show through the opaline. If you like the effect, fine; glue it in. If too much shows, give the glass another coat of opaline, let it dry, and try again with the foil. Foils come in many colors: gold, silver, pink, blue, etc. Foil Christmas wrappings are fine, or you can obtain some from your florist. After the foil is down tight, protect and seal with varnish, just as you did for paint.

Paper

If you plan to use tea paper, marbleized paper, etc., cut your paper

77. CENTER: *Swirled opaline clouds are painted over a ground of deep bronze foil glimmering through, on this large 20″ lamp set on a bronze base. Decoupage of hand-colored prints of hummingbirds and maidenhair fern. Top and bottom in brilliant vermilion, banded in green fronds. Maybelle Manning. In author's collection.* LEFT: *Two from a set of twelve glass coasters. Crumpled gold-foil ground with intarsia-like decoupage of marbleized paper in lapis lazuli, malachite and pink marble. Design taken from Ambassador's Staircase of Louis XIV at Versailles. Hiram Manning.* RIGHT: *This glass ashtray (one of the only two pieces of decoupage ever given to me) has a ground of gold leaf. Decoupage of Japanese flowers in Sanguine Palette. Designed and executed by Mrs. Clara Friedman. In author's collection.*

into "no-shapes," about the size of a quarter or fifty-cent piece as you did with foil. The shape doesn't matter, except there must not be any straight or pointed edges. Apply them the same as you would the aluminum foil, and be sure that every bit of glue and air is pressed out, as when you designed and glued your lamp. Clean off with a damp sponge, dry, and seal with protective sealer. Then varnish with two coats, and it is done.

Leaf

For leafing, silver or gold, you will need: Japan gold size, clear; leaf; two flat soft brushes, one-half inch wide.

The method is the same as for oil gold leafing, except it is done inside the lamp instead of outside on a surface. It is a devilish process, and I'd try plain oil gold leafing outside on something first,

78. *Pair of contemporary lamps, decoupaged on crushed gold-foil ground with giraffes and flowers cut from blank white paper. An example of folded paper cutting. (See Plates 23 and 24.)*

before I tackled this. Look under "Oil Gilding" in the chapter on "Gold Leaf on Gesso."

Gold Powder

For gold powder, apply a thin coat of Japan oil gold size to your sealed lamp, on the inside. Allow it to get tacky, and with a soft, flat, dry brush, "pounce" the dry gold powder onto the tacky surface until it is all covered. Brush off excess loose gold powder; let it dry, then proceed with foil as per paint instructions.

ASSEMBLING THE LAMP

One caution when having your lamp base mounted or wired.

Don't let the cap and base be screwed together too tightly, and make sure that the base and cap are a bit larger than the base and top of the glass itself. Glass, wood, and metal expand and contract at different rates, and wood and metal are tougher than glass. What happens if it's all too tight? The glass splits, ping, and there goes a lot of work! So mount them a bit on the loose side. Have your base weighted with lead or something to prevent the lamp from

79. Pair of glass lamps with ground of lapis lazuli paper, cut in clouds. Cartouches, on pinkish silver pleated foil ground, show figures of Louis XIV taken from the "Grande carrousel," the last tournament ever given. Top and bottom borders of gold braid and tortoiseshell paper. The Mannings. In author's collection.

ever tipping over from a strong gust of wind that might blow in the windows.

SUMMARY FOR DECOUPAGE UNDER GLASS LAMPS

1. Glue the cuttings inside the lamp, clean and dry the area; apply glass sealer to the glued edges.

2. Select a ground (i.e. paint, opaline, foil, paper, leaf or powder); apply as directed. If the ground is anything but foil or paper, foil must be applied to make it opaque. Let dry; apply sealer (except in case of opaline.)

3. Apply one coat of varnish, let dry; apply second coat of varnish.

4. Assemble the lamp.

PICTURES: ASSEMBLING, DESIGNING AND FRAMING

The technique for pictures under glass is almost the same as for a glass lamp base. The difference is its assembling and designing, and some of its backgrounds.

METHOD:

1. First of all, have your glass clean and have a piece of plywood or heavy cardboard cut the exact size of the glass. I use plywood, as it gives more protection to the glass and is easier to work on for some backgrounds. You will also need something to prop the glass up on so that you can get behind it with your hand. Depending on the size of your picture, this can be anything from a few old books to a cardboard box to a full artist's easel. I'll leave that to your own ingenuity.

2. Put your piece of plywood flat on a table, with your cuttings spread out on one side. Compose your picture on the plywood; tuck a rose in here, a leaf there, fern fronds, if it's a flower picture,

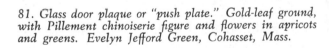

80. *Decoupage under glass with double frame; outside frame gold leafed; inner frame, with jet black ground, decoupaged with figures from print of Pompeiian ceiling. Picture under glass, hand colored in Full Palette, shows black-and-white Pompeiian figures on burnt orange velvet ground with Pillement flowers. Mrs. W. James Moore.*

81. *Glass door plaque or "push plate." Gold-leaf ground, with Pillement chinoiserie figure and flowers in apricots and greens. Evelyn Jefford Green, Cohasset, Mass.*

etc. It does *not* matter if pieces overlap. Your design and composition are what you are after. If you have the loose end of a rose stem dangling, tuck it under something in an effort to achieve the desired effect.

3. When everything is designed and placed to your satisfaction, return to your piece of glass and butter it on one side all over with all-purpose glue and water. Clean your hands and pick up the glass and lay it glued-side-down on your composition. Press gently with

your hands to get the composition to adhere to the glass. Then lift up the glass and turn it over, placing it face down on the table. You'll have a lot of loose ends dangling where you have overlapped flowers and such. Glue them down by lifting each piece and putting glue underneath and then pressing it down. Cut off really extraneous parts.

4. When the back surface is more or less glued, turn the glass over and prop it up so that the designs under the glass face you. Prop it up so that you can get your hand behind it to press and glue. Keeping your fingers moist with a damp sponge, roll and press from the center out to the edges with your fingers until every bit of glue and any air bubbles are gone and you can no longer see any glue move when you press from behind. Wipe off all the excess glue on the open parts of the glass with a damp sponge and let the picture dry. Then clean around the edges with your small piece of sponge wrung out in hot water.

5. When the back of the glass is clean and dry, seal it with glass sealer. For your background, you may use any of the ones I've described under glass lamp bases, or you may apply your ground to the piece of plywood which will back the picture in the frame. If you do this, seal the plywood first with protective sealer, and then you may paint it, gild it, cover it with paper, silk, velvet, or whatever pleases you.

6. Put the picture in its frame backed with the plywood, nail it in, and there's your picture. Take my advice and have a framer put it all together for you. He won't crack the glass and you might. And wouldn't you just love yourself then!

16 DECOUPAGE ON MIRRORS

MATERIALS

Colored prints sealed with protective sealer
Mirror (shock mirror, the thin kind)
Piece of thin glass cut the size of the mirror
Soft, black pencil
Flat toothpicks
Appliqué glue or glue of your choice
Bowl of water
Small piece of sponge
Tissue or paper towels

82. *Decoupaged mirror in two-tone gold frame. Design a combination of Pillement chinoiserie and singerie (see "Styles.") Mrs. Clara Friedman.*

83. *Ladies' hand mirrors (backs).* LEFT: *Venetian mirror. Ground of Venetian green, gilded handle and border with decoupage, in 18th Century Palette, of trophies and swags.* CENTER: *Early 18th century French mirror. Decoupage of baroque prints of tapestry designs on ground of black jade.* RIGHT: *English hand mirror. Decoupage of lush classic baroque prints on chrome yellow ground inlaid on reverse side in satinwood. Mrs. W. James Moore.*

Denatured alcohol
Cotton

METHOD

1. The first thing you do with the prints, before you cut them, is to take your soft *black* pencil and color the *back* of the prints black—and I mean *black!* This is to prevent reflection of the print from the thickness of the mirror itself; otherwise you will have white edges reflecting all over and your design will look as if its drawers had slipped.

2. Next, make sure your mirror is a shock mirror. It is the thinnest mirror made—what they put in ladies' pocketbooks. It is about one-sixth of an inch thick, no more. Get a thin piece of glass also, cut the same size. There are two reasons for the thinness: the thin

mirror reflects the back of the print least; and the thin mirror and thin glass make for less weight in the frame.

Go to your framer with the mirror and glass and ask him, when you select your frame, to have the rabbet cut or made deep enough to take them both. (He will give you quite an argument and can't or won't understand why you want a glass over a mirror. Just be firm, and if you feel you must explain, take a tip from the late Elsie de Wolfe, whose motto was, "Never complain, *never explain.*"

3. Let's suppose you now have the mirror, glass, and frame waiting for you at the framer's. Your prints are black on the back and now cut and ready to go. Place the mirror face-side-up on your worktable, cuttings to the left, glue, water, etc., to the right. Arrange your design of cuttings on the mirror, and when each piece is where you want it, mark the glass with a water-soluble glass marker at the top and bottom of a figure; the top, bottom, left, and right of a scroll, rose, etc. Just make a small dot on the glass, that's all. Then one by one, pick up the pieces of your cutting. Turn the cutting over and dab a bit of appliqué glue with a toothpick here and there. Don't put the glue at the edges; dab it in the middle of the back of the print. Turn it over, face side up now, and place it between the marked dots where it originally was. Continue so until all pieces of cuttings are in place and glued.

4. Remove any and all finger or glue marks, first with a piece of sponge wrung out in hot water and then with a bit of cotton moistened with alcohol, to remove any marks the water missed and to make the glass sparkle. Let the glue dry, then place the sparkling clear glass over the mirror and design. You can hold the two pieces of mirror and glass together temporarily with masking tape until you take it back to the framer's to have him put it in the frame and seal the back tightly with the usual brown paper. He by now agrees that you are not totally insane, and will ask you a million questions as to how you did it. And so will your friends! When you get it home, hang it, look into it, and I hope you see a satisfied smile reflected back from that mirror.

GLASS AND PORCELAIN MISCELLANY

POTICHOMANIA

This is probably the oldest form of decoupage known. But no one really knows. It was done on the outside of colored glazed pottery pieces, bowls, vases, urns, etc.; the inside was then still usable.

It can be done on any plain glazed ceramic surface, including porcelain. All you have to do is clean and dry the surface, apply a thin coat of protective sealer, and decoupage it. Varnish it, sand it, and wax it as you would any other decoupage for under varnish.

The original term is a French word meaning, literally, "pots in the Chinese manner." Phonetically, it is "po tee sho man ee," "po" like the southern "poor." All the syllables are evenly pronounced in French.

But just because it means in the Chinese manner does not mean you have to stick to Chinese or chinoiserie motifs. Decoupage it in mod if you like, or classic Greek, or flowers and butterflies—anything your heart desires. Just design it nicely, finish it beautifully, and you will have something unusual to put black-eyed-susans in or stick a lampshade on top of.

GLASS EGGS

This is another form of potichomania, as far as the technique is concerned. As to its history . . . well, people of all countries for a few hundred years back have collected and decorated eggs: ostrich eggs mounted in gold and silver; jeweled, decorated, glass eggs; gold and silver eggs; even semi-precious stones, such as the Russian Easter eggs or the Imperial Eggs by Fabergé which are unique!

Decoupaged eggs are just another form of this, and make utterly charming ornaments.

The technique is exactly the same as for any decoupage under varnish or a prepared surface. The only hitch is in the varnishing: you can only varnish half the egg at a time and you have to devise something to set the egg upon while varnishing. I make a stand

84. Potichomania. LEFT: *Chinese flower-holder in dark green glazed earthenware with deep yellow top. Decoupage of Pillement chinoiserie ships and flowers in Sanguine Palette.* RIGHT: *Rare small old Philadelphia glazed crock, now used as pencil and brush holder. Yellow-gray ground with decoupage of Boucher cupids, flowers, and swags in Grisaille. Mrs. W. James Moore.*

of modeling clay to set one end of the egg in while varnishing the other end, turning it only *after* that end is dry.

For preparing the glass egg, look up preparations of surfaces. You can paint it, gild it, anything. Then decoupage, varnish, sand, and wax as you would any other surface.

85. LEFT: *Potichomania lamp mounted in bronze doré. Ivory ground with chinoiserie decoupage in blue Toile de Jouy Palette. Mrs. James Powers.* RIGHT: *Wooden cylinder lamp in the Potichomania manner. Decoupage of hand-colored Persian flowers in Sanguine Palette on ivory ground, with teakwood carved top and base painted Chinese apricot. Miss Olivia Morrish, Boston, Mass.*

86. *A rare collection of Bristol glass eggs and their stands.* LEFT *to* RIGHT: *1. Grotesque brass stand with dragon holding egg; decoupage of Raphael prints in Full Palette on natural round. 2. Decoupage of Boucher cupids in Sanguine Palette with yellow, on lapis lazuli ground; Regency perfume-burner stand in lapis lazuli and gold leaf. 3. Pillement chinoiserie prints, in Pillement Palette, decoupaged on white ground. Antique Chinese base in dark bronze and gold leaf. 4. Baroque figures and chinoiserie scrolls on natural glass ground; bronze doré stand. 5. Decoupage of baroque prints shows "Europa and the Bull" against black jade ground. Silver stand, made from an old bun-warmer. 6. Pillement chinoiserie flowers, in Sanguine Palette, on Venetian yellow ground. Wrought iron polychrome stand in natural colors. Mrs. W. James Moore.*

Haunt antique shops, junk shops, or Aunt Hattie's attic for a stand to hold it once it is finished. Anything that will hold your egg up in style is "mist to your grill," but you have to use your imagination. One pupil of mine found an old beat-up silver-plated bunwarmer in a beautiful stand, ripped out the round bunwarmer, replated the stand, and presto! . . . an egg stand.

Glass eggs come in all sizes, from chicken size to the large economy family size. Hunt them up in antique shops. I really don't know which to tell you to get first, the egg or the stand. I guess the egg comes first, and then the stand to fit it.

BOWLS AND ASHTRAYS

Use practically the same technique as for lamps, above, except for the final finish, which is essentially the same as your regular decoupage finish under varnish.

Apply your design to the outside of the bowl or ashtray exactly as you would under glass, and finish it the same way, except that you eliminate the foil lining, Paint it, gild it, or cover it with paper. Clean and dry it, seal it, and proceed on the back exactly as if you were varnishing a regular decoupage surface. Sand it and wax it until it is smooth and glowing, and you may then use the inside or glass surface as a bowl, ashtray, or whatever suits your fancy.

SHADOW BOXES, VUE D'OPTIQUE, OR ELEVATIONS

MATERIALS

Shadow box or frame with glass
Thin sheets of cork or cardboard (I use both)
Appliqué glue; all-purpose glue; Duco cement
Bowl of water
Facial tissue or paper towels
Tweezers; small curved scissors; straight sharp scissors
Flat toothpicks
Long strips of plain white paper, 1½" wide, sealed with protective sealer.
Glass cleaner
Prints, with a thin coat of appliqué glue on the backs

This is a method of elevating any cut paper flowers, trees, leaves, figures, one over the other, to achieve a three-dimensional or optical effect. This can be anything from the shadow-box lid on a cigarette box to a six-foot picture on the wall. You may use flat prints, molded prints, or collaged paper-mache (see Index), or any combination of them, including pinpricking.

If you are going to make a large shadow-box picture, say with two or three elevations of collaged pieces, you will need a frame about two inches deep between the background and the glass. For smaller boxes or pictures with small scenes, the depth should be from a half-inch to one inch or more. This you will have to figure out for yourself. I will merely tell you the mechanics of it.

SHADOW BOX

Line your box lid with paint, paper, or cloth (see "How to Line a Box"). Have ready the glass which will fit on top of the box, flush

87. *Dancing the Polka: Godey print figures in collage. View from paper windows in vue d'optique. Note that flower details on gowns are pinpricked. Ground is blue brocade. Mrs. Clara Friedman.*

with the outer edges. Also get out the cuttings you plan to use which have had a thin coat of appliqué glue applied to the back of each. Use your finger to spread it as thin as possible.

You will now have to plan the design. The pieces which are to be used lowest in the design are pasted on one thickness of cardboard; those which are to be raised have several layers of cardboard. So the bottom pieces would have one thickness of cork or cardboard, the next layer two thicknesses, then three, and so on. My personal way of doing it is this: I glue one thickness of thin cardboard to the back of every piece and lay them and compose them *in* the shadow box, mentally figuring out which piece I want higher, which lower, etc. I mark the number of layers of cardboard I want on the back of each piece. I take them out and glue that many thicknesses of cardboard or cork on the back of

88. *Gold-footed shadow box for cigarettes; my most cherished piece of decoupage. Rocaille design of shells, ribbons, flowers and scrolls on silver tea-paper ground. Lid of pale blue silk serves as ground for bouquet of hand-colored flowers, strawberries, butterflies, bees and a fly—all elevated on pieces of cork. The last piece of decoupage made by Maybelle Manning.*

89. *Shadow boxes on gold tea-paper ground.* LEFT: *Elevations of Boucher cupids in paper-mache collage, with shaped leaves and flowers, in lavenders, pinks, and greens, on lavender velvet. Sides decoupaged with Raphael prints in matching colors. Mrs. Shephard Williams.* RIGHT: *Elevations of trees and "Lady in Swing," in 18th Century Palette, on apricot velvet. Sides in 18th century French figures and urns. Inside lid and bottom of box are also decoupaged. Evelyn Jefford Green, Cohasset, Mass.*

each marked piece and put them back in again, to find that I've goofed here, slipped there. So I either add or subtract a layer or two of cardboard or cork. There is no set way to do this, as each shadow box is different and no two minds conceive exactly the same design. My red rose may have three thicknesses of cardboard and yours two, or six.

I'll try and explain with a few sketches, see Figure 59.

Notice that each piece of paper overlaps the other and hides the mechanics of elevation. Suppose I want a rose, figure, bird, or whatever in the center partly on layer 2 and partly on layer 1. This

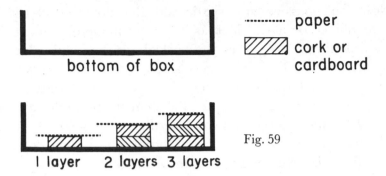

paper

cork or
cardboard

bottom of box

1 layer   2 layers 3 layers

Fig. 59

is how I'd do it: Between layer 1 and layer 2 is a lot of loose floppy paper that you can't glue to. I add pieces of cardboard or cork under them to make them solid and triumphantly glue my rose on top of my cardboard foundation, as in Figure 60.

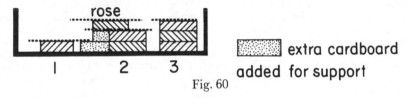

rose

1   2   3

Fig. 60

extra cardboard
added for support

Your cardboard or cork must never show. The piece must just seem to be there, elevated over the others, and the viewer must not be conscious of *how* it got there.

This is the way to glue the cardboard to the back of the print (Figure 61). The cardboard does *not* show.

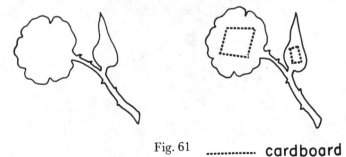

Fig. 61   cardboard

Now don't get overenthusiastic and glue down every last little leaf or ribbon, or it will look as if it were made of cement. Take those little tiny floaty pieces you backed with appliqué glue; twist and turn them with your fingers and tweezers until they appear natural. For a fern frond in a picture, you might tuck the stem under a rose and glue the tip of the stem to the underside of the rose. Then glue a piece or two of cardboard about three-quarters of the way up the stem of the fern, letting the tip float loose. This will anchor it but still let it appear loose and ferny.

90. Garden fantasy. A vue d'optique *combined with Godey prints of ladies and children done in collage and paper-mache. Sky of pale blue silk; everything else is paper; every last pink rose and green leaf is hand colored, and glued to white pasteboard trellises. Topiary orange trees in paper tubs consist of hundreds of hand-colored paper leaves applied one by one. Figures have every single flower and bowknot elevated, and they are collaged and molded in the round. Frame of tortoise-shell paper and gold bandings. Designed after the author's own chinoiserie garden; executed by Mrs. Clara Friedman.*

91. LEFT: *Oval box, ground of lemon gold leaf. A sentimental unique piece: colored by Mrs. J. Verser Conner, cut by Maybelle Manning (almost her last cutting), designed by the author, and signed by all three.* RIGHT: *Shadow-box bookends on Venetian green ground. Designs in Grisaille Palette on green silk ground, except for dark yellow designs used for the bases. Bookends are hollow, to hold pencils or flowers.*

Your composition is now assembled and glued-in firmly but airily. Turn it upside down, shake the daylights out of it, and maybe give it a few whacks on the table. Don't look at me with those great big eyes either, because if anything is going to come loose, *now is the time!* Or would you prefer to glue the glass on, passe-partout it, decoupage the outside, varnish it, rub it down, and *then* have it come loose?

Be sure there are no little loose bits of cuttings, strings of silk, dust, or whatever in the box. Clean your glass squeaky clean. Dab a bit of Duco cement around the top edges of the box, enough to hold the glass but not so much that it is going to squish out onto the glass or the inside of the shadow box. Place your glass on the glue surface, get it firmly into place, put a weight on it, and let it set.

Meanwhile, get your sealed paper strips ready. Cut strips a half-inch longer than each length of the top edges of the shadow box. If the box is two inches by four inches, cut two strips two-and-a-half inches long and two strips four-and-a-half inches long.

Remove the weight from your glass if it is set and glued firmly. Take some all-purpose glue and put a very thin coat on the back side of one strip of your sealed paper strips. Place this strip, glued side down, on the glass, even with the inside edge of the wood and just covering the edge of the silk lining of the box that is under the glass. Glue the strip down on the glass, being sure it is even at both ends. Miter the two ends from the outside edge of the box and glass to the inside edge of the box visible through the glass. Cut these with your small curved scissors and do all the sides of the box this way. Then glue the strip down over the edge of the glass, down on the side of the box. Your sealed paper strip is now evenly placed on top of the glass, forming an even frame for the shadow box, and glued down over the edges and sides. Pinch the edges of the strip, extending out from the corners of the box together with your two thumbnails and cut the edges flush with the upright corners of the box. Be sure they are glued tight.

Now cut another strip that will go all around all the sides of the box with one inch extra. Put a thin coat of all-purpose glue on the back and glue it all the way around the box with one edge flush with the top edge of the glass. When you have wrapped and glued it all the way around, pinch the two extending ends together and cut them flush with the corner. Then, if the sealed paper strip is wider than the side of the box and is extending beyond the bottom edge, trim it flush with your curved sissors. Press any edges down tight and wipe off any glue that may be present. Let dry.

Your shadow-box lid is now ready to paint to match the box itself, if it is painted, or to cover in paper if the box is papered.

92. *Group of three silk elevations on silk ground. Each petal in each flower a separate piece of colored silk, glued and shaped to form the flower. Mrs. Irving Wright, Milton, Mass. (Shown at the decoupage exhibit at the Wenham Museum, Wenham, Mass.)*

For a picture to hang on the wall all remains the same except the passe-partout part, though you can do it the same way and it gives a beautiful, simple frame for your picture. Or you can put your elevation in a regular frame that you have had made deep enough to hold the shadow box itself, and then hang it.

93. *A collage* vue d'optique. *Ballroom scene, with Godey ladies illuminated, collaged, paper-mache'd, and jewelled with real gemstones. All the flowers on gowns are pinpricked, as are scallops and small flowers. Background of blue brocade; view from window in* vue d'optique; *wall sconces in crystal; frame of tortoiseshell paper and gold bandings. Mrs. Clara Friedman.*

19 CARE OF DECOUPAGE

A piece of decoupage under varnish should be cared for, cleaned, and waxed periodically like any other fine piece. For waxing it, see instructions under "Waxing a Finished Decoupage." For a tray or tabletop, don't worry about drinks or rings—my finish, the maché varnish, is totally alcohol-proof. Finger marks or a glob of mayonnaise from the party can easily be removed with a damp sponge. Then re-buff the surface with a soft dry cloth, and if it needs re-waxing, wax it.

Don't place your piece in full sun. Even solid mahogany fades, you know. Raindrops on a windowpane combined with strong sunlight (like a sudden summer shower) can not only blister a piece but can actually set fire to a tablecloth or such. The raindrop acts as a magnifying lens to concentrate the sunlight to the point where it can actually char a piece of fine lacquer or a decoupage piece.

Every fine thing has its drawbacks. Venetian glass is very fragile; Sèvres and Meissen porcelain are hardly for the dishwasher; Waterford and Baccarat crystal chips if not handled correctly; and so does decoupage with a maché finish. It is completely alcohol-proof; heat, cold, and acid resistant; but give it a sharp bang and it chips. It doesn't dent; it chips, like crystal. In other words, little Junior can't bang on it with his little hammer. If by any ghastly chance he does, look up "Pitfalls, etc." You won't like it, but the cure is there.

Collage pictures are *not* for the seashore unless you are willing to have a dehumidifier as part of the deal. They will stand reasonable, but not constant, dampness.

How do you care for a lamp or any decoupage under glass? Treat the glass surface, and clean it, as you would a fine mirror or a piece of fine crystal.

Don't place heavy objects on a flat varnished surface such as a tray, tabletop, etc., until one year has passed, or the varnish will dent. After that, they are carefree. You see, it takes that long for the finish to set and completely harden. Varnish, *any* varnish, dries from the top down. The top may feel dry, and is, but way down at the bottom of the sea it is still tender, and that tender part will give if a heavy object is set on it.

If you treat your decoupage with reasonable care it will serve you well and long, but with a little *loving* care you'll get twice as much mileage.

Where the surface used is glass and the decoupage is under it in bowls and ashtrays, or outside it in potichomania, the glass surface can always be washed and kept clean as you would any fine piece of crystal. The decoupaged surface should be cared for as any other piece of decoupage under varnish. You cannot put these in a dishwasher. The decoupage will wash off.

L'Ouie

CARE OF BRUSHES

METHOD OF CLEANING

> Brush cleaner—an all-purpose one (see Sources of Supply) which cleans all goop off except lacquer or nail polish. For that you will need lacquer thinner.
> If you do *not* use all-purpose brush cleaner,
> For paint or varnish: Rinse brush thoroughly in turpentine, and then wash in cold water and soap until clean. Shape and dry.
> For protective sealer: Rinse brush thoroughly in denatured alcohol, then wash in cold water and soap until clean. Shape and let dry.
> For opaline: Clean in lacquer thinner or nail polish remover; it is the same thing and easier to obtain, then soap and water. Shape and let dry.

SHAPING AND DRYING

After the brush has been cleaned and washed in soap and water, the bristles or hair will tend to fly out sideways, giving the brush a splayed look. So, while the brush is wet after washing, run your fingers down it to press out the extra water, and lightly, with your fingers, turn the tips or edges of the flat brush inward.

For a pointed brush, point it with your fingers and then let it dry. Remember, the brush will dry in the shape you leave it to dry in.

Protective sealer, alas, seems to wreck brushes, and the bristles start to shed after a few times.

The best advice I can give you about brushes is *never* to let them dry before you have cleaned them. And remember that you can only do good painting or varnishing with a *clean* brush.

L'Odorat

PITFALLS, DISASTERS AND THEIR CURE

CHIPPED VARNISH

If varnish has been chipped as the result of a sharp blow or of being dropped, and a chip or piece has been knocked off but the decoupage design and background are not damaged, sand the flat surface surrounding the chip with No. 600 Wet or dry Tri-m-ite sandpaper and then with steel wool #400 to remove wax and matte final finish.

Then, with a small, pointed brush, put a drop or two of maché varnish in the chip and let dry. Repeat this until the hole or chip is completely filled and is a little above the original surface. Let it dry. Then sand with wet Tri-m-ite sandpaper starting with 280-A, then 400, then 600, then steel wool. Apply three thin coats of matte, twenty-four hours apart. Sand that with 600 Tri-m-ite sandpaper and then steel wool #400. Rewax it to match the original surface.

A BUBBLE OR LIFTED PIECE OF CUTTING UNDER VARNISH

Before I give you the cure, I'm going to tell you why it happened so that it won't happen again. After you've been through this cure I'll make a bet that you never will let it happen again.

There was not enough glue under that piece and that is why it lifted. Sure you put plenty of glue under it, but you probably had your sponge too wet or you failed to get the drop of water off your fingers when you were cleaning off the glue. As a result, the water ran under the glued print and leached it out to the edge. It appeared stuck, but was not. Don't do that again! Or you did not allow the glue to set enough before you cleaned it off, with the same result. I told you all this under "Gluing," but evidently somebody was not listening.

Now we get to the cure. Get out your sharpest X-acto knife and hone it, or use a new razor blade. With the blade on a sharp diagonal, all but flat against the surface, cut around the edge of that lifted print. Cut deep and surely, as if you were doing an appendectomy. Cut half to three-quarters of the way around the lifted print or bubble, then pull it gently back up. But don't crack it. With a toothpick, poke appliqué glue under it and on the partly bare surface. Press the piece back down and back to the uncut part, to squish the glue in there, and then back out to the cut edge.

When it is again flat, clean off the glue with a damp sponge. Let dry, and then you will have to remove the wax from the surface by sanding. Revarnish three to four coats and finish with matte final finish, exactly as you first started your decoupage, and the slit will not show (*if* you have done it my way from start to finish; otherwise I disclaim all responsibility!).

CRINKLED OR CRAZED VARNISH

If your varnish crinkles or crazes it means the coat underneath was not thoroughly dry. Don't panic and don't sand it. Just let it get bone dry, but *dry!* It may take from one to five days. When it is dry-dry, go on varnishing and it will be all right in the end, when it's sanded.

SANDING THROUGH VARNISH

1. I told you to stay away from corners.
2. Skimped on varnish, didn't you?
3. If you've rubbed down to bare wood and through the print, take a very small pointed brush, dip it into the original paint or

color, and put on just enough to cover the oversanded surface, no more. Don't flood it. Use a practically dry brush, and touch up the wood with the paint, blending it with your pinkie. Let dry, and apply protective sealer the same way. Let dry again, and then fill in as you would for chipped varnish, and refinish the same way.

4. If a print is involved and the raw edges of white paper are showing, get out the colored pencils. Pick one or two that seem the closest in color and a bit deeper, and a gray and a black pencil. Wet the pencil points in your mouth—don't use water. Get them good and wet, and touch the wet pencil to the frayed white edge of the paper. It will work almost like watercolor. Blend the color in. Don't press, paint it on, and relick the pencil when it is necessary.

If the color is too bright, it may be toned down with a gray or black pencil blended in. Get it as near the color of the rest of the print as possible, and if necessary use *every* pencil in the box the same way until it does blend in. Let it dry, dab a bit of protective sealer over it, let that dry, and then you can go on varnishing or revarnishing it. After all, the box is still at the sanding stage, so recolor, seal, and continue varnishing.

PEBBLING OR CONTRACTION OF A FINISHED PIECE

This can happen one to ten years later, or never, generally, thank heaven! Your piece was finished and rubbed down smooth as satin, and then one day it feels kind of grainy as you rub your hand over it. You stop and look, and the varnish is vaguely puckered, usually over a print. Reason? There is glue way down yonder that you failed to wipe off, or just plain missed, and it has pulled or puckered the varnish.

So drag out the sandpaper. Start with 280-A and follow the technique of sanding, as per instructions, until it is once again smooth and satiny. Reapply matte final finish, etc., as per those instructions. Wax it, and this time it should stay put, as the glue has already dried and will pull no more. Next time, clean the glue off the surface.

DENTS IN VARNISH

Remove wax (if any) from surface with turpentine and steel wool #400. Fill the dent with the original varnish, drop by drop, and let each drop dry. When the dried varnish is level with the surface, sand level as you would a newly varnished piece. Reapply matte final finish, sand that as per instructions, and rewax the whole thing.

BLOOM ON VARNISH

This is a funny cloudiness of surface, or bloom, that some varnishes develop. My only cure for that is to write the company or maker you originally bought it from. They will have the answer, or they certainly should. Maché varnish doesn't bloom, normally. If it is not properly waxed, however, it may. If so, wash it in mild soap and water, rinse, and wipe and polish it dry. And maybe break down and wax it?

Glue and Gluing Problems

DECOUPAGE LIFTING BEFORE BEING SEALED

Redampen it, run a little glue under the edges or any loose parts, and reglue it, pressing it flat down. Clean, let dry, and then seal it with protective sealer and put two, three, or four coats of varnish on it, one coat a day. You see, the protective sealer is not a finish and the glue needs to be sealed against moisture or against drying out too much.

GLUING OVER A VARNISHED SURFACE

Your decoupage may be completely or partially varnished, and then you find you've left something out, or something's come loose, or for some reason you wish to add another element. *Don't* just glue it on—rough the varnished surface with steel wool #400, glue down whatever-it-is, and go on varnishing.

UNGLUED COLLAGE OR PAPER-MACHE

Sometimes, in very damp weather (for instance at the seashore where they should not be in the first place), your collaged pieces may become soft or become unstuck from the ground. In this case, open the frame from the back and remove the glass. Remove the soft and unstuck pieces of collage and place them in the slowest oven possible, to dry them. Reseal, front and back, with maché varnish (two coats front, three back). Let dry, then recoat with matte final finish. Reglue them back into their original positions with appliqué glue, and they will be as good as new. This rarely happens, but I thought you ought to know how to repair it.

LOOSE VUE D'OPTIQUE UNDER GLASS

1. If it is a *frame,* your problem is small. Just undo the frame and reglue it, this time firmly, with plenty of appliqué glue which you obviously skimped on in the first place.

2. In the case of a *shadow-box lid* on a box, sealed with paper strips, etc., with the glass glued to the wood, and varnished, you can jolly well live with the loose bit; or, if it bugs you too much, take a *very* sharp, pointed, straight-edged X-acto knife or single-edged razor blade and cut through the varnish where the glass joins the wood on the top edge of the box lid. Cut gradually, but firmly. If you cut too quickly you will crack the glass. Gently ease and cut till the glass, varnish, paper strip (the whole bit) comes off and you can finally reach down inside.

Grab that loose piece, put *plenty* of appliqué glue on it, and re-glue it. Then glue the glass back on the top. You will have to give the cut varnished exterior a few more coats of varnish, rub and sand it down again, rematte it, and rub that. Rewax, and it's again as it originally was. But if the glass is cracked, you must start over from scratch, following directions under "Shadow Boxes."

CHIPPED GESSO UNDER GOLD LEAF AND VARNISH

Take an X-acto knife or a razor blade and scrape away a bit of the varnish and gold leaf on the flat surface surrounding the chip. Fill the chip with fresh gesso and let dry. Repeat till the fill is level with the surface. Sand smooth with dry 400 sandpaper. Seal with protective sealer (if it was oil gold leaf), apply gold size (Japan), and allow it to get tacky. Apply gold leaf, covering the scraped-off part also. Let dry, and fill in with varnish till it is level again with the old varnished surface. Then follow the whole sanding and matte final finish procedure. Wax, and if you've done it carefully, the chip won't show.

For burnished gold leaf it's the same, except that you don't seal with protective sealer, but reapply burnishing clay, etc. In other words, repair the hole from scratch. Unfortunately, the repair will show to some extent, but it will be better than a big hunk out of it.

If gesso shows small cracks like graining here and there under the varnish, well . . . it always has and it always will. It's part of it, like silver tarnishing.

A sharp quick blow or knock is what gesso does not like. It *chips,* and you are lucky if it chips neatly and you save the chips. You can glue them back in with appliqué glue. Press them firmly into place and wipe off any excess glue with a clean damp sponge.

WARPING OF WOOD

NEW WOOD

When decoupaging a new piece of wood, be sure to seal and varnish both sides. Varnishing on one side only builds up a tension and literally pulls or warps the wood. The varnish on the other side builds up a counter-tension and thus keeps the wood on an even keel. Even if you are planning to line a decoupage box in silk, give the inside a few coats of varnish before you glue in the silk.

If the box has warped, place the unvarnished side on a pile of damp, not wet, newspaper, about 15 to 20 thicknesses, and put dry newspaper on top of it. Then place a heavy weight, say an old sad iron, on top of that. Leave it for a few days, being sure the newspaper underneath stays moist. (I throw a sheet of plastic over it, and this helps to keep the paper damp.) When the warped piece is level again, let it dry *with the weight on it;* seal the unvarnished side with protective sealer; then give it two or three coats of varnish.

OLD WOOD

For old wood, if the piece is unfinished on the back or underside, do as above. If it *is* sealed or decorated, you will just have to scrape through part of it to raw wood, to allow the moisture to penetrate. Then follow the same procedure. It will just take longer.

If you don't wish to follow any of the preceding instructions, take it to the nearest cabinetmaker and see if he will consent to do it. Usually, he won't, and you'll end up with the old sad iron anyway.

Mind you, this does not always work, but I've had about 80 percent success this way, which is not a bad average. It will not work on large pieces. You need clamps and stuff *and* the cabinetmaker.

LAMPS AND GLASS PICTURES

If a piece of cutting comes loose in a lamp or glass picture, the reason is one of these: not enough glue; too wet a sponge that washed it out; or the paper was stretched and pushed instead of being rolled and pressed, and contracted back to its original size because there was not enough glue to hold it.

LAMPS: LOOSE CUTTING

For a lamp, the only cure is to take out the tired old X-acto knife and cut around that loose part right down to the glass. Lift it and reglue it with all-purpose glue (or whatever glue you used in the first place).

But before you glue it, replace it and see if any marks of cutting show. If the background was painted, touch it up with the same paint. Opaline? Do the same. Then reglue it and re-cover the inside of the lamp with foil. Reseal the slits or cut parts with varnish.

GLASS PICTURES: LOOSE CUTTING

On a glass picture, the process would be the same. I don't know what your ground is, but cut the loose piece out, reglue it, seal it, and reapply whatever ground it was you did use.

If your base is opaline, and it comes loose (although I've never known it to do so), cut down to it, reapply a bit of opaline, and reglue it in its own "juice." In other words, use no glue, merely replace it with wet opaline and let the old and the new combine and stick together. Opaline starts out white and gradually, through the years, will turn a pale tan-pinky color, like artificial pearls. This you can do nothing about; it is the nature of the beast. But it still remains lovely, like old ivory keys on a harpsichord.

BROKEN LAMPS OR GLASS PICTURES

You cannot repair the glass, but I can tell you how to save all or almost all of your cuttings, which you can then reuse in another lamp. Put the broken lamp or picture or pieces of them in a container large enough to hold them, cover with tepid to warm water, and let soak. This can take anywhere from an hour to a day. The foil will float away from the print. Then rerinse the print and remove any traces of glue or paint. Paint will "flick" off with your fingernail. Dry prints with tissue and let dry thoroughly. If they crinkle, they can be ironed. They can also be recolored where necessary and used again in another lamp or picture.

PAINT OR OPALINE RUNNING UNDER LOOSE PIECE OF DECOUPAGE

PAINT

1. Did not get it down tight, did you? Well—if it is paint, remove as much as you can around that spot, with a tissue dampened with turpentine.
2. Soak the loose spot with a hot *wet* piece of sponge—lift it.
3. Wipe off paint from front side of print and glass, again with a tissue dampened with turpentine. Dry.
4. Reglue with all-purpose glue and get it *tight* this time.
5. Clean glue off with damp sponge. Let dry.
6. Reseal with glass sealer. Let dry.
7. Proceed with painting in your ground.

OPALINE

Proceed as for paint, only using lacquer thinner or nail polish remover instead of turpentine.

TIN, METAL, TOLE

The only two possible tragedies that I can think of—outside of dents, chips, bubbles, etc.—are bent or dented metal and rust.

DENTS OR BENT METAL

Straighten it out as best you can, or have it done. The varnish will look like cracked glass and may be chipped. Fill the chips with the original varnish used, after you use the cure for chips. Then sand and give the cracked part two or three coats of varnish. Sand from the beginning all over again and apply matte final finish, following those instructions. Resand and rewax.

RUST

Well, I told you so, didn't I? So take out your X-acto knife, cut down through the varnish, paint, etc., right to the tin. Remove that rust spot and start from scratch, following the procedure I told you to follow in the first place. Now, look under "Preparing the Surface for Decoupage." Then repaint, revarnish, resand, rematte, resand, and rewax. And by golly, when you do another tin tray I bet you'll rustproof it first!

The basic thing I can tell you about repairs is to begin from the beginning and build it back up to where it last was before disaster struck, following the original process you used, using the same products you started with. For example, if you were using maché varnish, fill it with maché varnish, and if you were using varnish X, fill with that. Use the same glue, the same paint, etc. Successful repairing is basically using common sense.

Any time you get into some wild trouble not covered here, send me a self-addressed, stamped envelope with the question and room enough on the paper for an answer. I'll do my best to come up with a solution. (It could very well be *forget it!*) So, one envelope, stamped and addressed, one question, one answer. Fair enough?

22 CONCLUSION

To all of you who have read thus far through this seemingly happy-go-lucky presentation of decoupage, but who nevertheless realize, I trust, my great love and feeling of protective guardianship for it, I have this to say:

One of the most rewarding things in life is to create a truly beautiful work, whether it be a home, a garden, a painting, a chair, a mural, a cathedral, a matchbox, or a doorknob. *If* you have put integrity and beauty within it, it will be cherished and loved century after century, and part of *you* will be, too! How do you imagine works of art become art and are collected, cherished, loved, and preserved? It is because the person creating it put a big piece of his own soul (life, love, fun) and sense of beauty into it. This makes it live and gives the beholder a desire to own it so as to cherish and protect it from harm and preserve it for others to enjoy.

No piece of decoupage, mine or my pupils', has ever left my studio without leaving me feeling bereft, as if a child of mine had left home, and I fret and worry about each of them.

All of you who are *truly* interested in decoupage will find it one of the most rewarding experiences imaginable, as well as a great cultural education, for in some odd way it opens your eyes to things and objects you have looked at before, but have never really *seen*. You will find a whole new world of fun, beauty, and creativity spread before you that you had no idea even existed.

Self-expression is essential to any right-minded person, and a truly beautiful piece of decoupage, or *any* beauty that you have created, will give an inner glow to the *"you"* that brought it into being.

But never become satisfied; *always* go on learning and improving, because the day you think you know it *all* is the day you should look into the mirror and say, "I know nothing!" And that most certainly includes me!

94. *Queen Anne commode, one of a pair designed and executed by Hiram and Maybelle Manning for their godmother, Clare Boothe Luce, former ambassador to Italy. Commode on carved and gilded stand; top of green and gold paper inlaid in diamond pattern; front and sides decoupaged on silver leaf ground with camellias and maidenhair fern. Given by Mrs. Luce to the U.S. Embassy in Rome, for future occupants' enjoyment.*

95. *Decoupage can be a room too! Author's library entirely in decoupage on ground of Venetian green and Venetian yellow. Cartouches of gold-leafed carved wood. Design in Pillement chinoiseries of the "Five Senses of Nature," the four seasons, the four elements, and the arts. Over mantel, an original painting by Francois Boucher. Trays to the left are decoupage; mantel and hearth done in marbleized paper. Three top shelves contain "books" of cuttings. By Maybelle and Hiram Manning.*

GLOSSARY

A glossary of terms and names used either in the text or in
photograph captions and not fully discussed in context.

Bernini, Giovanni Lorenzo (1598-1680)—Italian painter, sculptor, and architect (see Plate 62).

bombé (French: rounded, convex)—As applied here, describes boxes or pieces
of furniture (commodes, etc.) whose sides or surfaces are molded in
swelling curves, mainly convex (see cover illustration).

bois de rose (French)—Rosewood, or a dusty-rose color known as such.

Boucher, François (1703-70)—Influenced by *Watteau* (see below); the most
fashionable French painter of his day, and a favorite of Mme. de Pompadour. Produced a vast number of pictures, decorations, tapestry designs
and fine etchings.

bronze doré—Gilded bronze.

burnish—As applied to the process of gold leafing: to give luster, make bright,
as opposed to *matte* (see below).

Canaletto, Antonio (1679-1768)—World-renowned Venetian painter noted
particularly for his documentary renderings of the canals and palaces of
the Venice of his day; a Canaletto print is used here as montage.

carrousel (French)—A tournament in which knights, in companies, variously
dressed, engaged in plays, exercises, etc.

cartel (French)—A frieze-panel; a frame, or a scroll. (*Frieze*—a band of
painted or sculptured decoration.)

cartoon—A drawing on stout paper as a design for painting, tapestry, mosaic,
etc. Also, of course (see "Biedermeier") an illustration in a comic paper
or periodical.

cartouche—A surround of a motif, usually with ornamental scrollwork—or
the cartouche and motif can be one, and surround itself, so to speak.

celadon—A porcelain ware from China, grassy-green to sea-green in color,
which has lent its name to similar colors used in decoupage.

Circassian walnut (see Plate 7)—Coming from Circassia, a region north of the Caucasus mountains on Northeast coast of Black Sea; corresponds roughly with modern Cherkess.

collage (French *colle:* glue)—A "glueing": various pieces of paper assembled and glued to form a design, literal or abstract. Not necessarily varnished. Decoupage is, in a sense, a collage.

Coromandel screens—So named because East Indiamen encountered the lacquer-work technique that makes the screens unique on the Coromandel coast, in Southeast India. There was a great demand for these screens in Western Europe toward the end of the 17th century. The design was cut out of the body of lacquer, and then completed in color or in gold. The typical designs were landscapes with pavillions and personages.

Cranach, or Kranach, Lucas the elder (1472-1553)—German artist and engraver. A friend of Martin Luther, he has been called the painter of the Reformation; his work is noted for freshness and originality, and for rich, warm color. *Cranach,* Lucas the younger (1515-86) continued his father's tradition; their work is often indistinguishable.

craze—To make small cracks on the surface, as of pottery or of a varnished finish.

Currier & Ives—American lithographers and print publishers, whose prints of contemporary scenes and events of American life during the last two-thirds of the 19th century have become sought-after collectors' items. Shown in this book as montage.

doyen (French)—A dean; the senior member of a profession, class, etc.; the one who has been at his job or post the longest.

Fabergé, Peter Carl (1846-1920)—Goldsmith-designer, jeweller and manufacturer, Fabergé was born in Russia of French descent. Among many unique specialties, he produced elaborately decorated boxes with surprises inside, notably, in 1900, the Great Siberian Railway Easter Egg. He created Imperial Easter Eggs annually for both Czars Alexander III and Nicholas II. Fabergé's masterpieces are noted for their exquisite workmanship and their imaginative ornateness.

Fête Champêtre—See *Watteau* below.

gesso—Gypsum or plaster of Paris, prepared with glue; a thick chalky liquid, used for covering up seams, joints, and rough raw wood, for sizing canvas, and as a base for gilding and painting.

Godey, Louis Antoine (1804-78)—American publisher, born in New York City; joint founder in 1830 of the *Lady's Book,* later known as *Godey's Lady's Book,* the first famous and successful woman's magazine: the source of the famous prints of ladies' styles of the period, unique of their kind.

Gould, Augustus Addison (1805-66)—American zoologist known for his bird prints and work on shellfish.

grain alcohol—Used in water-gilding; very expensive; the kind that's drinkable when diluted. Not to be confused with denatured alcohol.

grisaille—Monochromatic painting in shades of grey, often simulating sculpture; refers here, too, to a much-used palette for the coloring of prints, as elaborated and shown in text and illustrations.

intarsia (Italian: inlay)—A highly-developed form of wood inlay, originating in Siena, Italy, in the 13th century, probably derived from Oriental inlays of ivory on wood. It reached its zenith in 14th and 15th century Italy, remaining in use throughout the 16th century, and spreading to Spain, Germany and Holland. Designs, later utilizing a wide range of tones, included pictorial scenes and conventionalized scrolls, arabesques, and geometric forms.

Japan—A clear medium, similar to oil or varnish, that can be mixed with any color to give a hard gloss.

L'arte del povero (see "A Brief History" in text)—The Italian term for decoupage, meaning "the art of the poor man." Also known technically as *incisioni, minutaglia, ritagliati, applicati e laccato:* incisions, minutely cut, of bits and pieces, applied and lacquered.

marquetry—The application of a decorative surface of wood, or other substance, glued to an object on a single plane. As distinct from inlay, both field and pattern material are applied as a veneer of equal thickness. Derived from *intarsia* or true wood inlay (see above), marquetry occasionally makes use of tortoiseshell, ivory and bone. Used extensively by the Dutch in the 17th century; subsequently the French were its chief exponents, the foremost manufacturers being the Boulle family whose extensive use of copper and tortoiseshell created a distinctive style.

matte (French *mat*)—Dulled, deprived of luster or gloss, as opposed to *burnish* (see above).

Mogul (Indian: Mughal)—The dynasty that ruled in India from 1526 until 1858. Shah Jahan, who built the Taj Mahal, was a Mogul ruler.

moulage (French *mouler:* to shape or mold)—In decoupage, shaped or molded paper; a collage molded with *paper-mache*. (See *collage maché* below.)

opaline—Author's term for a painted ground (see "Lamps," in text) after the opaline glass that has a misty, pearl-like quality.

paper-mache (French *papier*, paper, and *mâché*, chewed.)—Paper reduced to pulp, mixed with glue, and shaped for molding into jars, trays, fancy boxes, etc. Another form uses paper strips or sheafs of paper glued together.

paper-mache collage, also *collage moulue*—As used in decoupage, paper prints molded onto a paper-mache base. If molded from the back, it would be called *repoussé*, see below.

Piranesi, Giovanni Batista (1720-78)—Italian engraver and architect. His copper-plates of the buildings and monuments of ancient and then-modern Rome number more than 1000, and are executed in a bold, powerful style. His architectural designs are notable for their grandeur and accuracy.

pointillism—The technique of painting in tiny dots of pure color, elaborated by *Georges Seurat* (1859-91), see below; a refinement on the broken color of the French impressionists just preceding him.

Redouté, Pierre-Joseph (1759-1840)—Luxembourg-born flower painter, draughtsman and lithographer, noted for his paintings and prints of roses. He painted all 170 plates for *Les Roses* under the patronage of the Empress Josephine from her extensive rose gardens at Malmaison.

repoussé (French: pushed back.)—See *paper-mache collage* above. In decoupage, a piece that is pushed out and molded from the back.

St. Non, Abbé de; Jean Claude Richard (1721-91)—French engraver, draughtsman and archaeologist. His four-volume work, *Voyage Pittoresque,* published in Paris 1751-6, contained 300 engraved plates.

scriban (French)—The art of decoupage, derived from the Italian *scrivania:* secretary desk, this latter having been an early decoupaged piece of furniture seen by French *découpeurs.*

Seurat, Georges—See *Pointillism* above.

Sèvres—Both a porcelain and its related colors. The porcelain is manufactured at Sèvres, France, and is of outstanding quality and costly to boot. Sèvres blue is of two kinds: the lighter blue, called *bleu celeste,* which is typical especially of pieces that antedated the French Revolution (1789), and the darker blue, called *bleu roi.*

shagreen—A species of untanned leather prepared from an animal's skin (horse or ass; shark or seal, etc.) and frequently dyed green. Also an imitation of this, or with an appearance similar to it. Seen illustrated here as the decoupaged (and montaged) covering for a trunk-turned-chest.

shot silk—Woven with warp-threads of one color and weft-threads of another, so that the color changes in tint when viewed from different points, giving an iridescent effect simulated in decoupage.

topiary—Describes trees or shrubs that have been trained, cut and trimmed into odd or ornamental shapes.

Turner, Joseph Mallard William (1775-1851)—English landscape painter. His early work rivals that of the great classical landscape painters; most of his Venetian paintings, however, belong to his last period, during which his color became stronger and his style extremely free and personal. Many of Turner's oils are treasured as masterpieces of English painting; in watercolor he is unsurpassed.

Watteau, Antoine (1684-1721)—French painter of Flemish origin. His small canvases, representing idyllic scenes of festivities in the open or characters from Italian comedy, place him among the great colorists of all time. *La Fête Champêtre* is one of his typically gay and sensuous scenes, all of which incorporate a profound lyric quality.

SOURCES OF SUPPLY

Boxes	Manning Studio of Decoupage
	Barbara Roth Designs, Inc.
Brass feet for boxes	Marie Mitchell's Decoupage Center
(ball and claw)	Local art and craft shops
Brushes	Art stores
(squirrel, badger, sable)	
Burnishing clay, Hastings	Art stores
Burnishing powder (gold)	Art stores
	(They may have to order it for you.)
Burnisher, agate	Art stores
Gesso	Art stores
Glass sealer	Manning Studio of Decoupage
Glue, etc.	Manning Studio of Decoupage
Gum arabic	Art stores (in small bottles)
Duco cement	Almost any store
Rabbit-skin glue	Good art and/or paint stores
(powder)	
Gold braid	Brandon Memorabilia
Gold leaf	Good art stores, Framing shops
Gold powder	Art stores
Gold size	Art stores
Modeling tools, wooden,	Art stores
etc.	
Opaline	Manning Studio of Decoupage
Lacquer thinner for it or	Paint stores
nail polish remover	Drug stores

Paint	Art or fine paint stores
Paper	
Marbleized	Good art stores, Framing shops, Decorators, Wallpaper shops and departments, Dover Publications, Inc.
Tea Paper	Good art stores, Framing shops, Decorators, Wallpaper shops and departments
Card or pasteboard	Art stores, Framing shops
Pencils, colored	Art stores
Prints, black and white only	Manning Studio of Decoupage Dover Publications, Inc.
Protective Sealer	Manning Studio of Decoupage
Sandpaper, wet or dry Tri-Mite	Hardware stores
Scissors, decoupage	Manning Studio of Decoupage Surgical supply houses Good cutlery shops
Sponges	Local supermarkets
Varnish Mâché Matte Final Finish	Manning Studio of Decoupage Manning Studio of Decoupage Manning Studio of Decoupage
Wax	Local stores
X-acto Knife	Art stores Craft shops

ADDRESSES

Brandon Memorabilia
222 E. 51st St.
New York, N. Y. 10022

Manning Studio of Decoupage
14 Wigglesworth St.
Boston, Mass. 02120

Dover Publications, Inc.
180 Varick St.
New York, N. Y. 10014

Marie Mitchell's Decoupage Center
16111 Mack Ave.
Detroit, Mich. 48224

Laverne International, Ltd.
979 Third Ave.
New York, N. Y. 10022

Barbara Roth Designs, Inc.
27 Upland Way
Verona, N. J. 07044

INDEX

[The color plates are reproduced on the book covers.]

D